PEOPLE POWER

Transform your business in the era of safety and wellbeing

KAREN J. HEWITT

Foreword by Louise Hosking, Director, Hosking Associates

People Power

First published in 2021 by

Panoma Press Ltd
48 St Vincent Drive, St Albans, Herts, AL1 5SJ, UK
info@panomapress.com
www.panomapress.com

Book layout by Neil Coe.

978-1-784529-52-9

The right of Karen J. Hewitt to be identified as the author of this work has been asserted in accordance with sections 77 and 78 of the Copyright, Designs and Patents Act 1988.

A CIP catalogue record for this book is available from the British Library.

This book is available online and in bookstores.

Praise for This Book

"This book dedicates a third of its excellent contents to the extremely important point that any efforts to change behaviors for health, safety and wellbeing, if they are to be sustainable and allow benefits to the business and employees to be realized, need to be 'baked' into company culture."

Katia Major, workplace wellbeing specialist and founder of Yoga Reading

"This book is designed to help you and your organization improve in many ways using health and safety as a core value and catalyst for business success and preservation of life. Karen has harnessed her many years of experience to create a roadmap to a better way of performing in an increasingly complex and fast-moving world."

Colin Lamb, experienced construction industry leader

"We are evolving every day to create enabled and engaged workplaces with empowered workforces. To do this we need to be inspired ourselves, and with this book, Karen has helped us to be so."

Benjamin Legg, Corporate Health and Safety Director, Ferrovial

"Karen's wide-ranging industrial experience comes out in this book in the form of a clear-to-follow recipe for successfully building an H&S culture in organizations at any stage of maturity. The chronology of steps for this recipe is well researched and well illustrated with stories and contributions from industrial leaders and subject matter experts, which is a testimony and credit to Karen's analytical skills and understanding of what makes humans and organizations tick."

Pierre-Arnaud Delattre, lead consultant, Value4Life

Dedication

For my daughter Mila.

You showed me that your dreams always find you in the end.

Acknowledgements

"You are the average of the five people you spend the most time with."

Jim Rohn

In the writing of this book, which took me the best part of a year, I was lucky enough to spend time (mostly virtually due to the Covid-19 pandemic) with some truly inspirational people in the field of business and health and safety. Some were people with whom I had worked extensively before and others I was working with for the first time. There is no doubt that the collaboration path I chose for the book enabled the process to be far better than it otherwise would have been.

And as I opened my writing project to more people, I specifically sought out more female voices, in the knowledge that they are still underrepresented – in the H&S industry specifically, in senior management roles in general, and even as authors of business books.

I want to thank every single one of the 15 contributors to this book, who generously gave their time and expertise, in the spirit of making a difference in our ongoing mission to keep people safe and well in our workplaces across the globe: Jason Anker MBE, Pierre-Arnaud Delattre, Ruth Denyer, Zoe Hands, Nicole Zerbel Ivers, Sarah Kerr, Colin Lamb, Ben Legg, Kirsty Mac, Ann McGregor, Monica Mesquita, Rob Owen, Karl Simons OBE, Ian Stevenson and Louise Ward. This book is so much richer for your experience and stories.

I was lucky enough to receive some insightful feedback when the book was still at draft stage, which helped shape the version you are reading now. I would like to thank Filip Coumans and Michael Colton in particular.

A huge thank you also to Louise Hosking for so kindly agreeing to write the foreword to the book and through this, providing readers with the benefit of her extensive experience in health and safety at work.

I could not miss this opportunity to thank my editor, Debs Syron, who got involved with this project at an early stage. As well as being a fabulous editor, she was a great sounding board for my sometimes crazy ideas.

And finally, to Mindy Gibbins-Klein and all the wonderful team at Panoma Press, my publisher, thank you for making this book happen.

On a more personal and logistical note, writing a book takes time, spread out over weeks and months. Without my partner, David, I would not have been able to bring up a beautiful daughter *and* write a book. Thank you for supporting my ambitions, always.

Foreword

By Louise Hosking, Director, Hosking Associates

This year it will be three decades since I graduated from Nottingham Trent University to embark on a career in environmental health. I remember being told, in my first week of lectures, that the work already undertaken by those who came before us to create safe and healthy places to work, decent standards of housing and safe food; to protect public health; and to reduce pollution, has saved more lives than any medical breakthrough.

However, despite all this history we have, at best, reached a plateau. Worldwide, ill health and injuries from work are still rising. Too many people are still dying or living with disability and illness due to their work.

It's time for a different approach.

Like the author, I support organizations to make health and safety a value in true balance with other business values, such as finance, sales and marketing. Even in a microbusiness, there is usually a plan for these business functions, yet health and safety is seldom viewed as a priority.

I have been asked to offer support in a wide variety of sectors where there has been no clear framework or direction for health and safety, yet the business has grown exponentially. By this point, it becomes the elephant in the room, viewed through a lens of being too expensive and too difficult. The reality for many is that health and safety is being placed in the time-consuming pile, so other priorities become more important.

But there is a good news story in this book.

The coronavirus pandemic has thrust a spotlight on to health and safety, and business leaders have stepped up to meet the challenge. A veil has been lifted and we can see just how interconnected we all are globally, nationally and within organizations – from the boardroom to the shop floor. By putting people at the front and center and going back to risk-based principles we will not just survive but thrive.

Health and safety is the ultimate team sport. It's a contact sport where we all have to be up close and personal. This takes honesty, introspection and therefore courage at every level.

For senior managers, this book contains a roadmap, a step-by-step guide, to help you achieve transformation and engagement from wherever you are now to where you aspire your organization to be.

For H&S professionals, this book will help you understand the motivations and distractions of your operational counterparts and help you define your roadmap from their perspective.

For human resources, marketing and communications teams, it will show how your expertise is crucial is supporting key messages.

At the end of each chapter there is a checklist and some action points to consider. These are equally relevant for those in global, medium, small and micro-organizations. It will also support those with supply chains that may reach into developing nations with few regulatory frameworks, where the starting point may be very different.

It provides thoughts, ideas and comments from H&S professionals, like me, who have seen the incredible impact motivated teams can have on the entire organization when we find its H&S sweet spot.

This book outlines a set of standard principles for leadership and engagement which can be applied to a multidisciplinary health, safety, wellbeing and resilience function or alternatively enable you to concentrate on a particular focus relevant at a particular time. In this way, it will help you shape your short-, medium- and long-term goals.

The author has been designing and delivering global programs for H&S engagement for the last 10 years and knows at first hand how to put health and safety at the heart of a business. Her early work was in marketing and communications, which glows from every page, and enables her to bring a unique insight to her approach. Karen is also a certified trainer of neurolinguistic programming, which gives her a powerful toolkit to create influential leaders who, in turn, put people first.

We support each other's work through our global H&S networks and via social media, especially LinkedIn. Women are underrepresented in our industry, but businesses are actively seeking out those with more feminine traits to solve problems and nurture inclusion. I was therefore delighted when Karen asked me to write this foreword for a book that champions this approach.

When health and safety is in balance, part of the DNA of an organization, and we focus on our people, it adds value to the organization. This book will show you how. When modern leadership is applied to organizational health and safety, it creates innovative teams who want to be there, who strive to do well for themselves and who do well for those who work alongside them. It builds psychological safety, and with psychological safety comes trust. When people trust each other, they bring their whole selves to work, can be themselves and can speak up because it feels safe for them to do so.

Health and safety gives organizations a common cause, or what Simon Sinek calls a "just cause," to sustain business over a long time.

It is time to throw out the clipboards; to thrive in the space between the black and the white and to start from a position of "YES!"

We are at a fascinating time in history. The decisions we make and those we choose not to make will be considered by generations to come.

You have chosen to make the decision to pick up this book, which means you are making a proactive choice to start a journey. This journey begins at the start, from where you are now with Chapter 1 – Dream: Imagine a safer company.

It really is going to take just one conversation at a time.

Louise Hosking, C.M.I.O.S.H., C.Env.H., M.C.I.E.H., C.Ma.P.S., P.I.E.M.A., S.I.I.R.S.M.

Director, Hosking Associates[*]

www.hosking-associates.com

https://www.linkedin.com/in/louisehosking/

---

[*]   This content has been produced by Louise Hosking, sole owner and director of Hosking Associates Ltd. The material has not been created in her capacity of president-elect of I.O.S.H., and communications being delivered here are in full representation of Hosking Associates Ltd only. Louise Hosking is not permitted to talk on behalf of I.O.S.H. Her I.O.S.H. role cannot be referenced without the express permission of the I.O.S.H. communications team. Thank you for your understanding.

Preface

I like to think about health and safety on a spectrum, from compliance to ownership.

Companies that do health and safety well balance both ends of this spectrum.

This book is *not* about compliance: it's about ownership – getting your people so fired up about health and safety that they lead it every day – and wellbeing, resilience and everything else in your business.

This book is your roadmap for boosting employee ownership of everything in your business, starting with health and safety.

Karen

@leaderlike

Contents

Introduction

Companies have been serious about health and safety (H&S) for decades

Health and safety has always been important to business. It takes us right back to the Industrial Revolution when the sad price of progress was measured in human life. Human beings were sacrificed, albeit not intentionally, in the name of industrialization and advancement.

When the Panama Canal opened in 1914, for example, it was the most advanced infrastructure project the world had ever seen, employing more than 40,000 workers over a 10-year construction period. Tragically though, more than 5,000 workers were killed in the process.

Over time, new legislation has been introduced, largely because of catastrophic events. Improvements have been made. The legacy of disasters such as Piper Alpha, where 167 oil and gas industry workers lost their lives in a series of explosions in 1988, is that it is no longer deemed acceptable for people to get hurt at work. Since then, the law has evolved to make sure that remains so.

If companies don't manage health and safety, and manage it well, lives are lost. This comes at an unacceptably high human cost, and a great financial cost too. Although the number of lives lost through workplace injury and illness has declined significantly over the last 100 years, companies and regulators agree that any life lost is unacceptable.

Even during the period from March 2020 to June 2021, when many people worked from home because of the coronavirus pandemic, there were still 111 workplace fatalities, according to the UK's

Health and Safety Executive (HSE). This was the lowest number of fatalities on record, but it was still 111 too many.

In 2016, industry regulators in the UK introduced new sentencing guidelines. According to the UK's Institute of Occupational Safety and Health these "have had a positive impact, persuading businesses to invest more in protecting workers, although more still needs to be done."

In 2019, the 10 highest health and safety fines were all over £1m, and the highest was as much as £5m. These fines were all issued to companies for failing to manage health and safety adequately, and some of these cases had tragic consequences.

Even before the pandemic, in the UK at least, it was deemed grossly unacceptable for a company not to do its utmost to prevent its employees from getting injured at work, or sick as a result of their work.

In 2020 this took on a new level of importance.

The arrival of the pandemic affected people and companies, all over the world. In the UK, at the time of writing, more than 128,000 people have died from Covid-19 (the disease caused by the SARS-CoV-2 virus) and across the world almost 3.5 million people have died from it. The human impact has been incomprehensible. The impact on businesses has also been severe. Simply to manage health and safety in 2020 and beyond, in addition to managing their normal risk profile, company leaders have had to:

- quickly implement new systems and procedures, to manage the risk that the virus poses to the health of their workforce, particularly for those who cannot work from home

- devise and implement new health and safety protocols for a workforce that is largely now working remotely and from home

- establish a cross-company response to a threat that is constantly changing and throwing up new challenges.

They have had to do all this, while also attempting to negotiate and mitigate against the economic consequences of entire industries being closed, for significant periods of time, as countries locked down to protect healthcare infrastructure and save lives.

By necessity, health and safety started to become a vital part of company culture, if it was not already.

'Health' was already vying for our attention

Occupational health had been calling for our attention for some time. According to HSE, in the year before the pandemic (2019/20), 1.6 million working people in the UK were suffering from a work-related illness. With a figure as high as this, reflecting so much human suffering, it is hard to understand why 'health' has long been 'safety's' poor relation.

The truth is that 'safety' gets our attention because it reflects the more immediate risk. A safety incident can happen in an instant, whereas a work-related disease usually develops over several years, so is easier to sideline. Conscientious companies have always given equal attention to 'health' and to 'safety', but companies that are less conscientious, less aware and more resource-strapped have not. That is until now.

Employee mental health and wellbeing were also becoming more important

HSE also estimated that in the 2019/20 period, before the pandemic, 17.9 million workdays were lost in the UK due to stress, depression or anxiety.

In the US, according to the American Institute of Stress, around 1 million workers miss work every single day due to stress. Annually, work-related stress causes 120,000 deaths and costs around $190bn in healthcare.

The scale and complexity of the problem was well documented by Stanford professor Jeffrey Pfeffer in his hard-hitting and aptly named book, *Dying for a Paycheck,*[1] (2019). Stress is a global problem, and according to the International Labour Organization, it contributes to the deaths of nearly 2.8 million workers every year.

Post-Covid, health and wellbeing, and psychological health and safety, are right up there with physical safety

Fast forward to a post-Covid era when health and wellbeing are now likely to be top of companies' agendas. According to Josh Bersin in his *HR Predictions for 2021 Report,*[2] the US corporate wellbeing market is worth more than $45bn and grew enormously in 2020. The report predicts that one of the questions on the minds of senior leaders in 2021 is "Do we need a chief health officer?" Whereas before the pandemic the topic of wellbeing was just beginning to emerge, it is now on full throttle, with companies' main concern being mental health. There is also a new ISO (International Organization for Standardization) 45003 standard on psychological health and safety.

According to the CIPD and Simplyhealth in their report, *Health and*

Wellbeing at Work (2021),[3] **more than two-fifths of businesses are 'extremely concerned' about the impact of the pandemic on employees' mental health.** The wide-reaching consequences of Covid-19 have taken their toll on people in so many ways. Grief, anxiety around the virus, lack of social contact, being separated from our loved ones, loss of confidence at work and financial concerns are all impacting our mental health. Where mental health concerns were an ill wind pre-Covid, they have now become a hurtling tornado.

Health and safety has expanded to include resilience

Josh Bersin (2021) cites 'resilience' as the word of the year. Resilience is defined as "the capacity to recover quickly from difficulties," and at no other time has this been put to the test as much as it is right now.

Savvy companies are turning to resilience to enable their employees to manage their own mental health better, thereby taking the pressure off their employer. After all, there is only so much that a company can do to help when it is facing its own pressures. Resilience is not a 'nice-to-have' quality for today's employees: it is a 'must-have.'

Even post-Covid, times are tough, and supporting employees to be more resilient is a win-win all around. Don't be surprised then, if you see health and safety functions adding both 'wellbeing' and 'resilience' to their remits. In fact, many already have; see for yourself when looking at the new health and safety job titles on LinkedIn.

The entire function is going cross-company

Looking again at Josh Bersin's findings (2021), it seems that the impact of health and safety in companies may be even wider than the topics we have already discussed. Despite the difficulties associated with the pandemic, it appears that declining engagement trends have reversed and are experiencing an uptick of late.

Furthermore, health and safety is now firmly linked to engagement, for better or for worse, and it is also venturing into its more modern form of 'employee experience.' Employee experience was already a cross-company affair, but what is different today is that the health and safety function is now a firm part of it.

What does the future hold for such an important topic?

They say that a rubber band, if stretched repeatedly, is unlikely to go back to its original proportions. The same is true of our companies. Having been forced to put health and safety at the center of their activities for months on end, doing so has become a habit. Employees are happy about this change; they now feel cared for and part of a cause.

It has taken a pandemic for companies, and their employees, to understand the critical role that health and safety plays in companies. Where there is a threat to public health, there is a threat to business, and without effective health and safety, there is no business.

The Covid-19 pandemic may have forced our physical separation, but we feel more connected to each other than ever, and this feeling has seeped into our companies. The pandemic has exposed our vulnerabilities. While having to live and work in ways we never previously imagined, employees and company leaders have been forced to show their human side at work. Work remains important, but people more so. Concerns for our health and safety have forced us to put people back in their rightful place, as the most important part of a company.

What is the new role of health and safety in the company?

As the pandemic recedes, companies are asking themselves the following three questions:

1. How do we continue to protect our workforce in the long term?

2. How do we engage employees, who have had their confidence levels knocked in the turbulence of a pandemic?

3. How do we get the best out of an employee base that is already having to operate in a 'new normal'?

And while these questions are being asked, and hopefully answered, the global health threat is still with us. As well as looking after their staff and protecting and caring for their people, companies must also engage them at the same time.

These are sizeable challenges, but what if there were a single solution to all of this?

Undoubtedly health and safety is a key driver of engagement

Neither engagement nor health and safety are new challenges, and both are fundamental to a company's success.

Arguably, engagement takes on the most relevance from an

employee perspective. Most employees, regardless of where they work, want to be engaged and to feel motivated. Before the pandemic, they probably would have ranked this far higher than health and safety. As for health and safety, most employees, unless they worked in the health and safety department, paid hardly any attention to the topic before, but they do now.

Now that employees, and entire companies, are taking health and safety extremely seriously, everyone is seeing the relevance of the topic. We are all taking it personally, because suddenly it *is* personal. Where health and safety was previously a remote, back-office function, famous for telling employees what to do and what not to do, it is now at the core of our very being.

This presumably accounts for the increased engagement levels discussed by Josh Bersin (2021). When employees feel strongly about a topic, have a vested interest in it and are part of a big and courageous effort to protect their work communities, engagement is not just pursued: it is a given.

Engagement creates culture, and for health and safety this means strong leadership from the top, role modeling from the middle, and ownership from the front of the company. Employees in a company that is truly engaged with health and safety don't wait for instructions to put it first.

This is the ideal scenario for health and safety, but what is the ideal scenario for engagement? What if there were a single solution to both?

Is it time to tackle engagement *and* health and safety together?

What is it that today's employees, and tomorrow's, really need?

There has never been a greater need for people to be cared for, shown empathy and looked after. Many companies have already risen to this challenge, but many have not.

Feeling safe is something we have all taken for granted in the past. What we know now is that without health and safety, life as we knew it before the pandemic can no longer exist.

Looking after our employees on a day-to-day basis is admirable, but now it is time for a long-term approach. This is the right thing to do for our people and it also makes good business sense.

The only way to do this is for health and safety to become our entire people strategy, rather than an, albeit essential, add-on.

It is time to recognize that health and safety is no longer a function that sits and works independently from the rest of the company.

Health and safety is something that impacts everyone, and it therefore needs to be owned by everyone. It is time.

Time to:

- put health and safety at the heart of companies

- convince other managers and the rest of our senior management team to commit to this

- get entire companies adopting simple everyday behaviors that create a strong health and safety culture

- provide us all with confidence that we can keep ourselves safe.

In this interconnected world, it is now clear that no one who takes a risk does so with consequences only for themselves.

It is also clear that everyone who takes protective action does so not only to protect themselves, but also to protect others.

The Covid-19 pandemic perfectly exemplified the above.

To the benefit of the entire company

When everyone in a community or a company puts health and safety first, we all benefit.

When employees feel safe, engagement levels rise, as people feel confident that their company cares about them. When engagement levels rise, so do productivity and innovation. This leads to reduced absenteeism, increased employee retention, more new business wins and enhanced company reputation.

So, at this point I am hoping that you are bought in and can see the benefits of putting health and safety at the heart of your company?

But you must be wondering *how* you can make this happen … right?

It is time for H&S leadership and H&S levership

What is H&S levership? This is when you use health and safety as a lever to transform your company.

The way to put health and safety at the heart of your company is to design, deliver and sustain a leadership program specifically for health and safety.

I know you probably already have leadership programs, but this one is different.

This program is for everyone, drastically increasing your levels of inclusion and employee people skills.

It is also a program that will repay its investment tenfold or more because it will create a culture that underpins and drives company performance. It is a program that will bring your company financial success, albeit not directly, provided that everyone sticks at it and does it properly.

As the change leader you are, no matter what job role or function you find yourself in, it is time to create an H&S movement in your company, and this book will tell you exactly how. Think of it as your roadmap to make it happen. The advice in it is not exhaustive, but it is fairly comprehensive. It references theory and research, but it is mainly practical advice, based on many years of experience. Every single page in this book reflects an action, opportunity or challenge that I have personally faced during the course of my work.

It is my hope that you will find the time to read the book from start to finish and use some of the content to make things happen in your own company. I also hope that you will put this book in a prominent place on your bookshelf, so you can pick it up from time to time and find the chapter that represents your biggest current challenge.

The checklists in each chapter are inspired by Atul Gawande and his book, *The Checklist Manifesto – How to get things right* (2009).[4] In the book, he discusses the success of the medical industry in reducing human error through the deployment of simple checklists. According to Gawande:

> They provide a kind of cognitive net. They catch mental flaws inherent in all of us – flaws of memory and attention and thoroughness. And because they do, they raise wide, unexpected possibilities.

There is a short story in each chapter, inspired by real-life events, although the names of the people and companies involved have been changed. There is also a comment from a health and safety expert, for a wider viewpoint.

Finally, there is a short action focus section, identifying one action per chapter for the different stakeholders involved in this lifesaving work.

I have divided the book into three sections: 'Build', 'Buzz' and 'Bake.'

I hope that these titles are catchy enough to remind you of the three important steps in this process.

So, now I encourage you to move forward with this change, and to use health and safety levership to transform your company and reap all the dividends that safety levership brings.

It is time for Part 1 – to BUILD the foundations for transformational health and safety.

PART 1

BUILD

CHAPTER 1

Dream: Imagine a safer company

Deciding to lead with health and safety, and now wellbeing too, putting them at the heart of our company sounds, on the face of it, like an easy decision. In reality, it is a tough call. We know that companies will succeed in the long term only thanks to their people. In the short term, however, the business imperatives of time and money usually get in the way.

The fact that we need to hold on to though is that caring for people makes good business sense. Yes, people and money go hand in hand, but only when we put people first. No matter how much technology and automation we introduce, there will always be a need for people. It is *their* skills that will either make or break the company. Even with the advent of artificial intelligence, the human brain can still do things that no computer can, and this makes our employees our most valuable asset.

When people are inspired, motivated and empowered, they stay resilient and healthy, whatever challenges they face at work. They follow the company's goals and put them above their own individual agendas.

When people lack inspiration and motivation, they often feel disempowered. They fail to take action; their productivity falls and sometimes they even get in the way of company progress. Never underestimate the loss of productivity caused by a disenfranchised employee, or the value that is added by an empowered employee.

For employees to feel empowered, they need a cause. They need to be working towards something that is important to them, feels relevant and gives them a reason to get out of bed in the morning. They need a cause that they believe in, one that demonstrates the integrity of their company's leaders. Fighting Covid-19 was everyone's cause during 2020, and that continues in 2021. Through health and safety, we can hold on to the positives that came out of this pandemic; the way it brought us all together, at and outside work.

When employees work for an employer who has integrity and makes them feel that they are part of something bigger and more important than just themselves, not only will they go the extra mile: they will run a marathon. This is worth its weight in gold in terms of employee engagement.

In summary, when we decide to put health and safety at the heart of our company, we do so for two reasons:

1. We know it is the right thing to do.

2. It makes great business sense.

Without both reasons being interlinked, our efforts to lead the company on health and safety may achieve early success but will falter when other priorities take over.

When we make this decision, we need to know what health and safety will look like when positioned at the heart of a company. Without a model for success, a blueprint for excellence if you will, it will be hard to convince everyone in the company of its importance.

What we need is a checklist for the new company we are going to create. Yes, we know we are about to transform our company through a focus on health and safety, but this is not necessarily something that we will want to advertise internally, and there is a very good reason for this.

Many people are averse to change, and even those who embrace it can get nervous about change that they consider too drastic and too quick. Having the rug completely pulled from underneath us is disconcerting, even when we are ready for it. While we prepare to create a *revolution* in our companies, we must remember that *evolution* is a lot more comfortable for most. We need to meet people where they are now and then lead them gently in our direction. We will still get the revolution we wanted, but in a much more calm and measured way.

Can you imagine *your* company with health and safety at its heart? With all the focus on people welfare that this will bring, what would you expect to see? There are a few things you will need to have in place before you begin, and this book will help you with all of them.

It will all start with a big vision, and even if we have to lead on this, we will still need our CEO and management to agree to it. They will also have to talk about it everywhere they go, even if they don't consider it to be a part of their role currently. The more our management team visibly demonstrates its commitment to health and safety, the more the employees will understand the importance of it and act accordingly.

Imagine then, a working day, week, month and year in our company. How will we create opportunities for our management team to communicate the importance of health and safety to our employees? How will their passion for employee health and safety be visible to employees, as often as possible, and across all the communication channels our company uses?

Once our management team starts to be visible regarding health and safety, employees will start to change their behavior. H&S rules will already be in place and now all we need is for our employees to follow them. We also need *them* to let *us* know if the rules aren't suitable or workable. How else will we know what needs to change?

There can of course be a missing link in the chain: line managers and supervisors. Even if our employees receive the messages coming from above, they can be forgotten instantly if their line managers don't reinforce them or, even worse, say the opposite. Line managers and supervisors are the key influence on their teams for everything, including health and safety, so their engagement is crucial.

Nothing missed by an evangelist

Duncan was managing director of a construction industry materials supplier. He knew that he needed to get his supervisors driving health and safety at his worksites. His senior leadership team were all on board with the safety message and were talking about safety to their workforce at every opportunity, but they didn't appear to be getting the message. He was still hearing stories about people taking shortcuts, every time he made a visit to one of his yards, and the reports of near misses were coming in far too often for his liking. The supervisors just didn't seem to want to get involved, and even worse, they were often the ones who were taking shortcuts. Enough was enough; Duncan had to make a change.

He decided that the supervisors would now be the ones delivering the safety message, instead of the H&S person on site. When his supervisors started evangelizing about safety, that is when Duncan could be sure that he would now get the safe company he wanted. As the adage says, "There's no better way to learn something than by teaching it." This strategy worked a treat. Not only did workers stop taking shortcuts, but the supervisors' level of motivation seemed to have gone up a gear, and they were more productive as well.

This is why a company with health and safety at its heart will be more joined up in terms of both messaging and behaviors. Where links in the chain are missing, the H&S culture will break down, with potentially life-threatening consequences.

Imagine a set of dominoes all lined up on the floor in front of us. We have taken the time to get each of the dominoes into position and measured the right distance between them. We are sure that the first domino, when pushed, will knock down the rest of them in turn, right up to the final domino.

This is how we want our H&S transformation to work. One action or behavior sets off another, and another and another, until every single part of the company is doing the right thing and moving seamlessly in the same direction.

A domino effect essentially relies on two things: an initial action and the subsequent momentum. This momentum will continue as far and wide as we have people, provided the correct alignment is there. In practical terms, this means that we need everyone to sign up to the message and to the same behaviors.

In large companies, communication has a long way to travel, and this distance comes with a huge potential for error. Communication of our H&S message must, in some global companies, travel across borders and cultures. It therefore needs to be as simple, translatable and culturally transferable as possible. If we achieve this well, we can prepare to marvel at just how well our message travels.

In a company where health and safety comes first, managers know what 'good' for health and safety looks like. Now we just need to make that happen.

⏻ Checklist 1

Defining a success model for the health and safety led company

1. An ambitious vision for health and safety that everyone knows about and buys into.

2. A CEO who evangelizes about health and safety wherever they go, whatever they talk about, and at every meeting.

3. A management team that takes every opportunity to talk about health and safety.

4. A set of H&S behaviors that are meaningful to the company, based on an analysis of H&S incidents, and are well communicated.

5. Line managers and supervisors who role model the right H&S behaviors.

6. Employees who take ownership of health and safety by following the H&S behaviors and rules, and politely challenging others who don't.

7. Employees who come up with and implement their own ideas about how to make their workplaces safer.

8. An H&S department that monitors and measures its success, including how well the required H&S behaviors have been adopted.

9. An H&S message that permeates the whole company and is embedded in daily processes and activities.

 Action focus 1

For senior managers:
Get your management team together and brainstorm your excellence model for health and safety success in your company, based on Checklist 1 above.

For health and safety professionals:
Consider point 8 of Checklist 1 above, and how you currently monitor and measure your success in the company, identifying and closing any gaps.

For the communications and engagement manager:
Consider point 9 of checklist 1 above and identify available channels for cross-company communication.

For the human resources (HR) director:
Consider how H&S leadership might be linked into your HR processes and any generic leadership programs and initiatives.

Colin Lamb, experienced executive board leader

In a construction career spanning five decades, I have been lucky enough to work in some highly respected, dynamic, and forward-thinking companies and to develop a real passion for health, safety and wellbeing.

When I look back on how the industry has evolved to meet the changing needs of society and technology over those five decades, I am struck by just how far we have come in striving to protect people from harm. There are many personal and industry-wide stories from the trailblazing days of my career, when an H&S culture was the collective aim, but not always the reality. Today, we can see a paradigm shift from lip service to real caring.

When I consider what a company with a passionate focus on health and safety looks like, I realize that these companies have people who believe in safe work methods and avoiding harm to people as their primary obligations in fulfilling their role.

Companies that have a fervent belief in health and safety, as well as the emotional intelligence and persistence to succeed, have always been high performing. They have prospered in competitive industries, where a point of differentiation can be difficult to achieve, and have enjoyed a high level of respect from the market. This has brought them more commercial success than companies that have been more complacent about health and safety.

The company with health and safety at its heart has a different mindset from others. It is driven by positivity, creative thinking, transparency of data and good communication. It is supported by flatter company structures and strong leaders who walk the talk. When this kind of company pursues improvement in H&S performance, measured in numbers of H&S incidents, it makes sure that it takes a balanced approach to data, recording both safe and unsafe behaviors and conditions, and learns from it.

The language used here is important. Talking of 'learning events' rather than 'near misses' has enabled H&S-focused companies to empower employees to seek solutions to H&S problems, without fearing blame. H&S conversations on site have also been made easier through this balanced approach. They have become a game changer in enabling H&S-focused companies to reap the benefits of improved H&S performance.

Another thing you can expect to see in a company with health and safety at its heart is tidiness. This may seem trivial, but it is not for nothing that many people say, "A tidy site is a safe site." In my five decades of experience, companies with tidy workplaces are not only safer, but also more profitable and happier places to be. When employees take pride in the way their workplaces look, they take pride in everything. As Henry Ford wisely said, "Pride is what happens when no one is looking." This is true, because with pride, employees are happier and work effectively without supervision. This goes some way to explain why companies that create pride around health and safety are more successful.

CHAPTER 2

Vision: Define your long-term goal

We have decided to lead our company health and safety first, and we now have a pretty good idea what success looks like, but where do we start?

In *The 7 Habits of Highly Effective People* (1989),[5] Stephen Covey sets out seven habits to strive for in order to be highly effective, as per the table below. Even today, these habits are still much quoted and discussed.

The seven habits of highly effective people

Habit 1 – Be proactive.

Habit 2 – Begin with the end in mind.

Habit 3 – Put first things first.

Habit 4 – Think win–win.

Habit 5 – Seek first to understand, then to be understood.

Habit 6 – Synergize.

Habit 7 – Sharpen the saw.

As you can see, the second habit in the list is "Begin with the end in mind." In effect, we have already done that, having imagined what a company with health and safety at its heart might look like. We have defined our destination. Now we need the vehicle to take us there.

This requires a vision. We need to formulate our overall objective, so that we can communicate it to the rest of the company. What is it that we want to achieve?

Let us think about this for a second. What we want, surely, is for every one of our employees to go home from work safe and well, every single day. We want a workplace where no one is harmed or becomes unwell due to the working environment, ever. This is the utopia. The reason why H&S professionals get out of bed to go to work every morning.

Some people call this 'zero H&S incidents,' while others call it 'zero harm.' The term 'zero' has certainly gained some traction over the years, probably from the inevitable focus on incident reporting and recording. Whenever we record numbers of unwanted events, the obvious target is zero.

No one should ever have to feel the pain of an accident or long-term illness at work, for themselves, for a colleague, for a friend or for a loved one.

For this to be possible, everyone in the company needs to look out for everyone else. For every incident that ever happened, there was nearly always someone who saw it about to happen, who could have stepped in and stopped it. We need to understand *why* they didn't and *what* would have to change, so that next time they *would* step in, without thinking.

To achieve this we need to inspire, enthuse and motivate the employees in our companies about health and safety. We need to get them so fired up about it that they don't think twice about acting to keep their colleagues safe and well. We need to get them so confident that health and safety is the right thing to do, that they step up and act as H&S leaders. But how can this be done?

H&S leaders *always* adopt healthy and safe behaviors themselves. They report hazards, unsafe acts and behaviors. They speak out when they perceive a risk. They set the example, for instance, during the Covid-19 pandemic, following government health guidance by wearing face coverings and social distancing. It sounds easy, but it is easier said than done, especially in traditionally 'macho' working environments.

In fact, there are many barriers in a company to employees stepping up to be H&S leaders. This is why we need a vision, and an effective one. A great vision is the first step in removing the barriers to H&S leadership in our companies. It is our vision that will keep employees motivated day in, day out, no matter what else is going on.

Our vision will create motivation for health and safety that lasts not just months, but years. We need to understand first what a vision is, and then how we can make it a great one.

The foundation of every successful H&S leadership movement is vision, and it is worth taking the time to make sure that:

- we have the right vision

- the whole management team buys into it.

This is important because wanting success is not enough. We need everyone else to want it too, especially when conflicting pressures make it difficult for employees to stay focused.

To work, our vision for health and safety needs to motivate the whole company into concerted action towards it, continuing over the long term, regardless of the internal and external distractions.

Health and safety is the toughest of missions because it is often relegated down the list of priorities when pressure from cost and schedule arises. Will health and safety still be at the forefront of employees' minds when the threat of Covid-19 has been eliminated? A decision to stop work for health and safety considerations can be very costly, and this makes employees hesitate. Employees may also hesitate for other reasons, and these will be discussed later in the book.

A strong vision, however, will cut through all of this, and keep every employee focused on health and safety, no matter what problems occur. When a vision is strong it acts like the North Star, guiding employees, keeping them on track and showing them the right thing to do. The North Star shines brightly, lighting our path when the way ahead is unclear.

In *Our Iceberg Is Melting*, (2017),[6] John Kotter outlines eight steps to achieve successful company change. He tells these through a compelling fable about penguins at the South Pole. His eight steps have been tried and tested in many companies with great success.

In the third step, he talks about "creating a vision for change." He argues that employees find it easier to let go of the status quo, once they know what their company's future is going to look like.

John Kotter's eight-step change model

Step 1 - Create urgency.

Step 2 - Form a powerful coalition.

Step 3 - Create a vision for change.

Step 4 - Communicate the vision.

Step 5 - Remove obstacles.

Step 6 - Create short-term wins.

Step 7 - Build on the change.

Step 8 - Anchor the changes in corporate culture.

In *The Infinite Game* (2019),[7] Simon Sinek talks of a "just cause," which he defines as "a forward-looking statement that is so inspiring and compelling that people are willing to sacrifice to see that vision advanced." Health and safety is the 'just cause' that our companies need today.

Not all visions, however, are formulated in a way that allows lasting change. A vision needs to be written in a certain way and getting this right will be the single most important factor in achieving our H&S ambitions.

The right H&S vision has the potential to unleash the H&S leader in all of us.

It is a simple statement, the words of which need to resonate with everyone in the company.

A well-formulated vision provides a goal so big that employees can constantly strive for it and feel proud to be a part of it.

This vision needs to be formulated at the highest level of the company. H&S leadership might be for everyone, but it becomes a movement only when it starts and is driven from the top.

So where do we start? How do we write this vision?

For most companies, a vision is usually a very generic goal. It is a statement of how the company wants to be, or what it wants to do, in the future.

For health and safety, and arguably for any successful vision, this goal needs to be formulated in a specific way. It is a formula I call ALTE, which stands for 'Ambitious', 'Long-term', 'Towards' and 'Emotional'.

A – Ambitious

Have you ever heard the words of John F. Kennedy, when he wanted to inspire Americans to get behind his vision of putting a man on the moon? What he said was, "We choose to go to the moon in this decade and do the other things, not because they are easy, but because they are hard …"

It was the ambitious nature of his vision that inspired people to get behind it. Putting a man on the moon was so ambitious that it broke the bounds of possibility, and this is what Americans found hugely exciting. The same thing happened when NASA landed a robot on Mars in early 2021. The whole world was watching, glued to their televisions to see it arrive, and revel in this incredible human achievement.

Our employees will be inspired by thinking that the seemingly impossible might be possible, and that they could be a part of it. That they could be a part of something that no one else has ever done before. They could be part of a team that achieves a first in history – something that leads the way for others to follow.

L – Long-term

No ambitious vision is ever going to be achieved quickly. If it were, then it wouldn't be a vision at all, at least not a particularly ambitious one. Anything achieved in the short term has to be a goal, rather than a vision. Another reason why our vision needs to be long term, in that it takes a long time to achieve, is that we also need to keep our employees motivated for a long time. We may never achieve our company vision, but if it keeps our employees focused on health and safety every single day, then it is a strong vision indeed.

T – Towards

Any goal we want to achieve in life has two ways of being formulated, and to a certain extent, the language we use will depend on how we are motivated. Human beings are generally motivated either by moving away from something we *don't* want, or towards something we *do* want.

Imagine if we decided to embark on a new fitness regime. We may tell ourselves that we want to stop putting on weight or, couched slightly differently, we may say that we want to be healthier.

Both are our vision for success, but the words of the first one are 'away from' and those of the second are 'towards.' This is because saying we want to stop putting on weight, is us moving away from what we *don't* want. Saying we want to be healthier, is us moving towards what we *do* want, towards being healthier.

There is no right or wrong here, and both serve to motivate the formulator of the goal in the short term. In the long term, however, only a goal that is 'towards' will keep us motivated, because it keeps us constantly moving in the right direction. The 'away from' goal causes us to lose motivation the moment we start to make progress in moving away from the thing we don't want.

Does this help to explain the concept of yo-yo dieting? Or in health and safety terms, why we experience waves in our H&S incident trends and why we find it hard to make the targets we want stick? With both examples, we are successful one minute, then lose traction the next.

When it comes to health and safety, this knowledge is critical, because we don't want peaks and troughs in our incident trends. We want constant progress in keeping our people safe.

I hope this explains why our vision for health and safety needs to contain words that move us and our employees towards what we want, rather than away from what we don't want.

E – Emotional

There is one final ingredient needed for a strong vision. It needs to be emotional. We like to think of ourselves as logical creatures, especially in the workplace, but we should remember that human beings don't make decisions based purely on logic. All of us, regardless of personality, make decisions based on a combination of both logic and emotion. There is probably a larger element of emotion in our decision-making than we like to admit.

When we present our vision for health and safety, we must do so with great fanfare, so that it will touch people's hearts.

Our emotions naturally come to the fore when we are asked to be involved in something that has never been done before. We also react emotionally when something is hugely important to all of us. Health and safety is, of course, relevant to everyone, as we are all impacted by it. The challenge is to make sure that our employees know and understand this.

I have a dream!

Sarah had been tasked with getting her whole company behind the wellbeing message, and she knew this had to start from the top. The company's CEO was very supportive and talked about wellbeing wherever she went. She also encouraged her executive team to do the same. The trouble was that there was no vision for wellbeing, and Sarah knew that without this, it would be hard to get the enthusiasm she needed from the employees. In the end, she realized that there was an easy solution.

When Sarah was writing a message from the CEO to be recorded on video, it occurred to her that this was the perfect opportunity to present a vision, with real purpose and presence, that made sense for the company. Echoing Martin Luther King's famous public speech, "I have a dream," the CEO's message began with "I want our company to be the first to put mental health on a par with physical health." This was a bold vision for the future, and one that made a real impact on the employees watching it, throughout the whole company.

Three years later, after a full roll-out of the wellbeing program, it transpired that the CEO's vision was the message that employees were most able to recall of all the company messages they had received during that time.

The formula is simple, as we have seen. Here are two examples of ALTE visions for health and safety:

1. Be the safest company in our industry.

2. Be the reference company for health and safety in our industry.

Both visions were formulated by real companies that were very successful in transforming themselves, through a focus on health and safety.

Can you see why? Look for the ALTE formula in these statements.

Creating and broadcasting an ambitious vision for health and safety is where the transformation starts. Now it is time to create a business case for putting health and safety at the heart of your company.

⏻ Checklist 2

How to write your vision for health and safety

1. Write a statement describing the company you want to be.

2. State it in the positive – what do you want?

3. Write it as a state you want to reach in the future.

4. Make it ambitious – something few companies, if any, will achieve.

5. Make it ethical – something that is the right thing to do.

6. Make it a goal that will take a long time to achieve.

7. Make it something that isn't easy to achieve.

8. Think about how you will know when you have achieved it.

9. Keep it simple and memorable – so that every employee will be able to repeat it.

 Action focus 2

For senior managers:
Get your management team together and come up with an ALTE vision for health and safety in your company, based on checklist 2 above.

For health and safety professionals:
Draft your own version of the ALTE version, based on Checklist 2 above, and use it to influence your management team.

For the communications and engagement manager:
Consider how any H&S vision might work with company brand and tone of voice.

For the HR director:
Consider the role of HR in fulfilling any vision for health and safety.

Ian Stevenson, executive project director

Health and safety impacts everyone, because wanting to care for one other is a fundamental human characteristic. When things go wrong and people get hurt, we feel their pain, even if we don't know the people concerned. In my life, major incidents where people got hurt or sadly lost their lives, have had a big impact on me. I am thinking of the Aberfan disaster in Wales where so many schoolchildren died. I am remembering the Ibrox disaster, where many football fans lost their lives on a stairway in Glasgow. I am also thinking of the terrible Piper Alpha disaster in the North Sea, where 167 people died. The saddest thing of all is that all these disasters were avoidable.

I have been an advocate for health and safety for many years. Managing health and safety well means ensuring that a company can manage its operations in such a way that the risk of hurting someone is as low as is reasonably possible. It also means that a company has minimized the possibility of its own life-changing event happening. We need to make sure that our Aberfan, our Ibrox, and our Piper Alpha never ever happens.

The people who create the operating environment – the management team, the workforce and suppliers – all need to consider their collective and individual roles in the H&S management of our operations.

Many years ago, the company I was a part of had a poor H&S record. It was operating in a highly hazardous industry and there had recently been a spate of fatalities. The CEO then took the bold decision that this loss of life could no longer be tolerated. Not only that, but he wanted his company to become the reference company for health and safety in its industry. This would mean that not only would no one get hurt, but also that everyone would go home safely, every single day.

This was a laudable ambition and was brought to life through a dedicated H&S leadership program, relaying transformational leadership behaviors from management to middle management, and down the chain to the workforce. It enabled the right conversations on health and safety to take place regularly, and it taught employees how they could communicate better and how to lead on health and safety.

And the result? Everyone got behind the CEO's incredible vision and, over time, their H&S culture and their H&S performance changed for the better.

CHAPTER 3

Commitment: Get all management on board

With a vision for health and safety in place, and now wellbeing too, it is time to make sure the entire management team is on board. Of course, they may say they are, but we need to be absolutely sure.

Whether you are in the management team already or part of the health and safety function, getting management on board is crucial, because it takes a long time to change a company's culture to a health and safety led one, and we need to know that they won't falter at the first hurdle. We all know that companies can be driven by short-term results, but as we have seen, a dedicated H&S program is a long-term endeavor. It doesn't mean that we can't find some quick wins, as we saw in Step 6 of John Kotter's eight-step change model in Chapter 2, but staying power is going to be important.

When the management team questions the impact that the H&S leadership program is making, reassure them by saying something like this:

> Making sure that our people, and those impacted by our activities, go home safe and well every single day is not something we can do one day and not the next: it needs our constant focus and attention. The moment we let our guard down and become complacent is the moment someone will get hurt or fall ill.

In the model of cultural maturity for health and safety (Parker et al., 2006),[8] the above mindset corresponds to the fifth and final level that every company aims for, but very few, if any, ever reach. It suggests that companies in this category – called 'generative' – exist in a state of healthy paranoia. This is therefore not something that companies need *to do*, but something they need *to be*, every single day.

Although this model predates the Covid-19 pandemic by some 15 years, 'healthy paranoia' is a fair description of what we lived through during the pandemic, although at some moments it may have felt more like hypervigilance.

This is why what we call our H&S focus is also important. Call it a program because that is what it is. But it is vital to make it clear to everyone involved that it is a program without end. For as long as there are employees in our company, there is a need to keep them safe and well. Focusing on this and living permanently in a state of healthy paranoia is highly effective. Those who tell us such a program is too costly (and you may share this fear) should be constantly reminded that it is also, quite simply, the right thing to do.

Using the terminology of program can be useful to us, allowing us to plan, set out a timeframe and establish resources. Make sure that you plan for a continuous roll-out, albeit with an initial three-year plan, a review of progress at the end of it, and then a continuation plan for three more years.

I use the number three arbitrarily, because only you will know how long your initial planning period needs to be for. For large companies, three years is about right for reaching the entire workforce with the first round of training. It is also no mean feat to reach hundreds or even thousands of employees globally. But with the right approach, our H&S culture change will begin to happen. For smaller companies, a program like this will be rolled out much more quickly, and the challenge then will be sustaining it, as we discuss in Chapter 14.

We need to imagine our H&S leadership program as a waterfall. It takes just one drop of water to get it started, but many more to get the water moving in any kind of volume. Once it is moving, however, it will be hard to stop. This is momentum, and it is what we want our program to achieve. The momentum needs to be constant, so that the success becomes self-sustaining and part of our company's DNA.

Having got to this part of the book, you (the reader and change leader) and I (the author and change advocator), are already those first two drops of water that your company needs. All we need to do now is understand how behavioral change can become a waterfall.

When we speak to other managers about our plans, they may try to convince us that it is only the frontline employees and workers who need to adopt the right behaviors for health and safety. To some extent, they are right. After all, it is the frontline employees who often face the biggest risks to their health and safety, and who represent the last line of defense. They are the people who can stop an accident or illness happening, or alert managers to someone showing signs of worsening mental health.

What this conclusion misses, however, is that in large companies, no behavior happens in isolation. A company is a system, or a series of mini systems, where individual behavior is influenced by the behaviors of the people around and above them. Peer pressure is strong, and so is pressure from further up the company.

In this context, employees will take their lead from these four things:

1. What other people are doing around them.

2. The physical environment and what behaviors this facilitates and drives.

3. The behavior of their immediate line manager.

4. What they perceive to be most important to the company.

We also need to remember that we want everyone in the company to act as a leader for health and safety. They will do this only if they are sure that they will have support from their line manager and from management. No one will stick their head above the parapet if they might end up getting it shot off in return for speaking up.

Changing behaviors is never easy because we are creatures of habit, and habits run extremely deep. When it comes to health and safety, however, this is the easy part. Employees *will* change their old habits for new when they are given a good enough reason to do so; when they get time to practice them; *and* when they see that their bosses are doing the same.

The hard part is getting employees to challenge others who are not adopting the new habits or who are continuing to behave unsafely, for whatever reason. Asking them to intervene brings up perfectly understandable fears: fears of offending someone, of appearing stupid, or of being blamed by management.

While intervention for health and safety comes from a place of good intention, unless it is approached with care, the person on the receiving end may not see it that way. They may feel judged or blamed if the language and tone is not right. After all, how many of us enjoy being called out for our behavior, even if it is done kindly? Not many, that is for sure.

For all these reasons, and even though the H&S function may be the natural 'owner' of this kind of program, success will be ensured only when we have first 'sold it' to the rest of our management. What this means is that we need to provide the business case for leading the company health and safety first. With so many strategic areas to focus on, why should management choose health and safety? And why should they listen to *you*?

They should listen to *you*, dear reader, not because you tell them that putting health and safety first is the right thing to do (they know this as well), but because you are going to give them a comprehensive and compelling list of reasons, which explain why the company should invest in a dedicated program for health and safety. Why leading the company health and safety first is not just sensible, but a complete no brainer. And here is that all-important list:

1. **Legal protection for the company.** If there were an accident in our workplace, the ensuing investigation would check that we had done everything in our power, or the legal term is 'reasonably practicable,' to prevent an incident. If we hadn't done this, we could be sentenced and sanctioned accordingly. So, let's make sure our corporate consciences are clear.

2. **Better H&S culture and performance.** When we demand a focus on health and safety and H&S leadership from everyone in the company, we build a culture that reduces the likelihood of

anyone getting hurt. Over the years, an increased focus on health and safety should correlate with a trend of declining incidents, all other things being equal.

3. **Increased engagement and productivity.** A focus on health and safety at all levels of the company will lead employees to feel cared for, which will make them feel more motivated and engaged. This in turn will lead to increased productivity, reduced staff absenteeism and increased employee retention.

4. **Reduced costs.** The safe way of doing an activity is very often also the right way of doing it. When employees do a job the right way and follow the defined work method, they are getting it done right first time. There is no waste or duplication, and if this is a task that is repeated over and over, it could add up to a large cost saving for the company over time.

5. **Better client relations and more business wins.** Companies with a strong focus on health and safety and a good H&S record inspire customer confidence. This boosts reputation and leads to more contract wins.

6. **Better supplier relations.** Extending H&S leadership into the supply chain reduces incidents and illnesses, and enhances supplier relations. This means projects are completed on budget and on schedule, which boosts both companies' performance.

7. **Stronger culture.** H&S leadership throughout the company is a vehicle for building a strong H&S culture, but it doesn't have to stop there. The H&S leaders it creates are prepared to do the right thing, not just for health and safety, but for everything else in the business. They act as role models, exemplifying the right way of working across the board. With their newfound communication and leadership skills, they go on to improve the culture of the company overall.

How can I afford not to?

Eduardo had created quite a buzz around his new H&S program, and the H&S function couldn't wait to get started. They were champing at the bit to roll out the new messages and training to their part of the business. Before they could do that though, they needed to sit down with their bosses and get their buy-in. It didn't matter that the corporate division had already given the go-ahead, because the individual divisions liked to make up their own minds. They wouldn't budge unless they thought it made sense for their division. After all, they were accountable for their division's successes, and its failures, and this couldn't be one of the failures.

To help the H&S managers sell the idea to their own bosses of leading health and safety first, Eduardo developed a presentation for them to give. This made clear all the reasons why a focus on health and safety would be good for their business. This compelling business case then paved the way for a full-scale roll-out of Eduardo's program. No more did they hear "What will it cost me?" only "How can we afford not to now?" Where some managers might have blocked a program like this in the past, they were now completely behind it. Within three years, the investment had paid off: the culture was much improved in all divisions, and they were reporting fewer incidents.

Assuming that all the management team members have bought into the many benefits to the business of a focus on health and safety, all that's left is to create some urgency around the need to change, as per Step 1 of John Kotter's change model mentioned earlier. The sense of urgency is created by an acceptance that things can no longer go on the way they are, at least from a health and safety perspective. Even if our company has never had a health and safety incident, at least not one that had to be reported to the relevant regulatory authority, it has undoubtedly experienced near misses.

Whether you decide to make this case for urgency before or after you talk about the benefits, the case needs to include information about where the company is right now on health and safety, and why it is not acceptable to do nothing or to accept the status quo. The statistics we present will depend on the internal data we have available to us about health and safety in the company and will range from concerning incident trends to a deep dive into an incident or miss that shows the urgency of the need to act. It is particularly useful to analyze near misses because they often show the potential for something far more serious to occur.

If we don't have enough data on health and safety in our company, we can look at accidents that have occurred at other companies in the same industry, or in a different industry but at a company undertaking similar types of work activity. What's important here is that we build on the benefits of putting health and safety first, as we mentioned earlier, with the warning that if we don't, it could cost us dear in terms of human and financial impact.

Today's health and safety is certainly quite different from the old-fashioned sense of the term. In fact, it is one of the functions in a company where the rubber really hits the road, because leadership in health and safety requires the strongest of all people skills. To be bold, brave and to stand up for what is right. These are skills that once embraced will spill over and benefit so many other areas.

This is why H&S leadership, when done well, becomes a trojan horse for change in a company. It is the reason why, when our employees show us that they can be leaders in health and safety, we know they can be leaders of anything.

Health and safety is far from being a dry duty that companies perform just because they have to. It has become their secret weapon.

Make sure that your whole management team is armed with this knowledge and prepare to install H&S champions in all the right places in your business.

 ## Checklist 3

Key elements of a business case for a focus on health and safety

1. It protects people, property and the environment, and ensures that everyone who is affected by the company's activities, goes home safe and well every single day.

2. It reduces incident and illness rates in the company and boosts H&S performance.

3. It reduces cost and waste as people adopt a safer way of working, which is also usually the right way.

4. It increases engagement across the company, as employees start to feel excited about the mission, and understand that they work for a company that really cares.

5. It increases employee retention and decreases absenteeism.

6. It enhances productivity, because when employees are more engaged, they work more efficiently and effectively.

7. It boosts reputation, as our company will be perceived as having integrity.

8. It brings in new business, as other companies want to work with a company which does the right thing, by setting and upholding new standards.

9. It creates goodwill on your company balance sheet, as your H&S program becomes a valuable company asset.

 Action focus 3

For senior managers:
Based on Checklist 3 above, consider how successes in health and safety can be correlated with successes in other areas of the business, for example, customer satisfaction, productivity and quality.

For health and safety professionals:
Draw up a presentation that sells the benefits of a focus on health and safety.

For the communications and engagement manager:
How can you provide a measure of health and safety engagement in any existing employee engagement surveys?

For the HR director:
How will you link increased levels of engagement in health and safety to employee retention and absenteeism levels?

Rob Owen, chartered health and safety practitioner

When making the business case for health and safety to management, I keep in mind a principle that applies whenever you want to influence anyone to buy into anything: "What's in it for me?" (WIIFM). For your management team, with their business hats on, 'WIIFM' becomes "What's in it for the company?" (WIIFTC). It is up to you to get the answer across.

To convince management to focus the entire company on health and safety, and to lead health and safety first, I ask myself what WIIFTC means to a senior leader. It is often couched in terms of the benefits that this approach will bring to the business. How will it help improve our efficiency and our effectiveness? How will it reduce our costs or improve engagement, productivity and performance? This is really the same approach you would take if your management team were your customer, which they are.

Making a pitch for a significant investment of time and resources in health and safety is no different from selling to any other company customer. Making this investment has to provide value to the business.

Health and safety as a product has an additional and highly compelling unique selling proposition. Its primary aim is to reduce harm and ill health to all employees and those affected by the operation. This is quite simply the right thing to do. It is also a legal obligation. What is very interesting is that leading the company with health and safety may require significant investment, but the return on that investment will be even greater. It will improve not only H&S performance, but *all* performance, because when employees can lead health and safety, they can lead everything.

Management may be on board at this point, but they may also be concerned about the disruption this change will bring to the business, because as the saying goes, "You can't make an omelet without breaking a few eggs." You will put their minds to rest, by showing them that you have planned well and that you will be able to keep disruption to a minimum.

Finally, your management team will be delighted if, as well as presenting an excellent business case for a company focus on health and safety, you can also show that you intend to align your approach with existing processes and initiatives. You might then put your final 'ball in the net,' with a couple of great examples of where a similar approach has paid great dividends, in another company or industry.

CHAPTER 4

Sponsorship: Install champions in the right places

We have decided that we want our company to put worker health and safety first.

We have also developed a bold and inspiring vision and got the whole management team on board; so far so good.

Now we need to do one more thing to set ourselves up for long-term success. One thing that will help us to ride out the peaks and troughs of keeping the company engaged around health and safety. One thing that will give the workforce influence when the going gets tough.

We need to get an H&S professional on our executive board or management team. Furthermore, it can't be just any H&S professional, but the most senior one we can find. I know this sounds as though it might get expensive, but all it means in practice is that in an ideal world, our H&S director, or you if you are the H&S director, needs to sit on the executive board or be in the management team.

Putting the H&S director at the top of the company gives proper recognition of the place that health and safety holds in our company. Recognition of its top status, alongside other business-critical functions such as sales, finance, HR and procurement. Without this, some people in the company may question how committed it is to the issue. Also, management commitment is *key* to our health and safety success. When the commitment is there, this will be visible, and indeed obvious, to all.

There is another important reason why we need our H&S director to operate at the highest level. Sooner or later, we will come up against a conflict in our endeavors to put health and safety first. As you will probably have already noticed, there is a natural conflict between H&S and other departments in every company, for example, between H&S and production, H&S and cost, and H&S and schedule. When we look at what we have learned from the Covid-19 pandemic, there was a conflict between health and safety and everything we had taken for granted, including going shopping and out to pubs, clubs and cinemas.

Sooner or later, someone will say the following, when workers are feeling empowered to insist on certain health and safety measures:

> "But we need to get this job out of the door by [insert pressing deadline]. The client won't take no for an answer."

OR

"But that's too much money; we need to do this as cheaply as possible, or we won't get the contract."

OR

"But we can't close down the plant. It'll cost us too much money."

OR

"That all sounds great, but who's going to pay for it?"

OR

"We just need to get this job done, or we won't have jobs ourselves by the end of the week."

Do any of these phrases sound familiar?

There are things we can say, and questions we can ask, to counter these kinds of objections and get people thinking differently. Sometimes however, we don't have time for any of this, especially if lives are at risk.

There will be times when health and safety issues need to be escalated, because employees are not getting the results they want, and the people around them just aren't getting it. When we can escalate health and safety issues right to the top of an organization, we can be sure that we will get the right result.

In an ideal world, everyone will be acting as an H&S leader, which means putting health and safety first, *no matter what*. In most companies, however, this is a utopia, a long way off. When people start to put health and safety first in our companies, no matter what, and are prepared to make tough decisions, then we know we are beginning to make headway.

If it is not possible to put the H&S director on the board or in the management team, there are still other ways to ensure that health and safety gets the attention that it deserves.

Usually, the conflict between health and safety and cost, production and schedule comes from the operational areas of our business, so this where we need health and safety reinforcements.

Does it make sense to create H&S champions among our operational leaders, so that any conflict disappears before it even gets to management?

Having the H&S director on the board or in the management team is the most reliable way to ensure health and safety always comes first, but going the H&S champion route is another good option. If we have both options available to us, then we have the potential to transform our culture faster.

Whether the H&S director is at the top of our company or not, we can create operational H&S champions by nominating one of our management team as the company 'H&S sponsor.' This should be someone who demonstrates a passion for health and safety and will therefore champion its cause at every management meeting.

Next, we can nominate an H&S champion, who should be one of the most senior operational leaders, in each of our operational areas or divisions. These are the people who will dictate and create H&S culture in their parts of the business, regardless of what is mandated from above.

This network may be small or large, depending on the size of our company. Whatever the size, it is important to cascade it down through the company, creating a hierarchy of H&S champions who are there to support employees and the H&S professionals, if the operation isn't giving them the support that they need.

When creating this network, make sure that each H&S champion has all the credentials of an H&S leader. They need to feel passionate about the topic first and foremost, with many years of experience and exposure to health and safety. They also need to have plenty of health and safety related anecdotes, with appropriate lessons that have been learned, to tell others.

Everyone needs a champion

Ellen was seeking a way to elevate health and safety in her company. The H&S director was a big supporter, but he wasn't on the management board, and she got to speak to management only once every quarter. The operational part of the business was the place where all the health and safety incidents were being reported, but the local health and safety teams often found it difficult to escalate issues when they occurred.

Ellen decided that she needed to get reinforcements at operational level, outside the health and safety teams. She asked the H&S director to lobby for the MDs of each business unit to nominate a member of their leadership team as their H&S champion. From then on, when H&S issues were escalated, the H&S champions stepped in and provided their backing. This transformed attitudes and led to a far better health and safety record. And guess what, the H&S director got his place on the board.

The H&S champions also need to evangelize about health and safety at every opportunity.

Our operational H&S champions need to be prepared to speak out for health and safety, and to take tough calls when they perceive that there is a risk. This may not be a job for the faint-hearted, but it has great potential to transform health and safety for the better.

Finally, each H&S champion needs to be a role model and lead by example. Wherever there is an H&S rule, they need to follow it. This means at work, outside work, and on the way to and from work. Every minute of the day we are influencing people by our behavior, even when we think no one is watching. For health and safety, this influence must always be positive.

All this role modeling and leading by example means nothing if it is *invisible* to the rest of the company.

The H&S champions, if they want to influence others to behave safely, need to take every opportunity to make their commitment to health and safety *visible*. It is no good them wearing their commitment on the inside; they need to have it tattooed on their foreheads.!

Joking aside, there are many ways for H&S champions to visibly demonstrate their commitment to health and safety. Examples include conducting regular H&S tours; building H&S moments into their team meetings; and showing up at training sessions for the H&S leadership program that we are about to launch.

When this network contains the right people doing the right things, and we have made clear to them what these 'right things' are, success will be guaranteed. Health and safety will start to be owned not just by the H&S function, but also by the operation itself.

As the original change leader, an MD or senior manager, or a member of the H&S team, you may be leading health and safety now, but it's the operation that will lead it for years to come.

So, fasten your seatbelt and get ready to define the H&S leadership behaviors you are going to need.

⏻ Checklist 4

Questions to use to select the right H&S champions

1. Are they operational, that is, non-H&S specialists?

2. Are they passionate about health and safety?

3. Do they have some great stories, lessons learned and personal experiences about health and safety to tell?

4. Do they talk about health and safety all the time, and inspire others to listen?

5. Do they role model the safe way of working – at work, outside work, and to and from work?

6. Do they make their commitment to health and safety visible?

7. Do they ask their workforce what they think about health and safety?

8. Do they involve them and ask for their ideas?

9. Are they prepared to stand up for health and safety and make tough decisions to keep people safe and well?

Action focus 4

For senior managers:
Free up senior operational people to be advocates for health and safety.

For health and safety professionals:
Produce a RACI** matrix outlining the operational health and safety champions you require and how they will support the function.

For the communications and engagement manager:
Provide training in public speaking to the chosen H&S champions.

For the HR director:
Find a way to recognize H&S leadership talent and integrate it into the existing talent management activity.

Nicole Zerbel Ivers, corporate health and safety director

The key to getting the entire company committed and engaged in your H&S system is to have top management committed first. Championing health and safety starts at the top of an organization. I know that sounds like a cliché, but it's true. I have worked for a number of firms, but the leaders at my current one are the most authentic and actively committed to health and safety of any I have worked with. The difference this makes is *huge*.

** A diagram that outlines the extent of the involvement of key stakeholders in a project. RACI stands for Responsible, Accountable, Consulted and Informed.

The top leader must understand the health and safety goals and how we will achieve them, then communicate them to their direct reports, and finally hold them accountable for achieving them. They in turn must set health and safety goals for their own direct reports and hold them accountable for the same. When top leadership goes out to a jobsite, they need to assess what they see through the lens of health and safety, just as they traditionally did for production.

Getting all the above into place is easier said than done, because not everyone is a natural H&S leader. Many people want a safe project, but not so many people know what behaviors are required to achieve this or how best to communicate them.

This leads me to my second point about H&S champions: coaching and guiding your leadership team for health and safety is the second most important point in your plan. Coach your leaders on practical H&S activities, where they can be visible to employees and really make a difference, for example, leading a stand-down, a safety meeting or a site management walk.

Coach them on how to engage with the workforce, especially the contractors. In practical terms, this may mean giving them a list of suggested questions to ask, such as "Can you tell me about your job, and what is the most hazardous part of what you do each day?" or "If someone were to be injured today on this project, where or how could it happen?"

The above two points are important, because you can have the best written H&S plan in the world, but none of it will happen unless the workforce understands what their leadership team and supervisors want and expect for health and safety, and crucially what they will hold them accountable for. This may require metrics and performance assessments. A few years ago, in a previous company, we set a goal to get all our employees OSHA (US Occupational Safety and Health Administration) trained but struggled to get them to attend. We then tied the goal to their bonuses. Guess what? We met it.

Sometimes companies don't communicate the actions needed behind their words, thinking that if they repeat the phrase "health and safety first" enough times, it will magically be so. For sure, saying "health and safety first" is a great start, but to make it a reality takes deliberate effort and relentless messaging. It means managers understanding the expectations, knowing what to do, and being held accountable, all the way through the company. This is why you need a network of H&S champions in your company. They are the key to getting an entire company leading health and safety first.

CHAPTER 5

Behaviors: Define the safe actions you need

We have started planning our dedicated H&S leadership program – the one that is going to transform our company – and we are already thinking big. We have an ambitious vision that proves it. We are confident that this vision will keep all our employees engaged around health and safety, for many years to come.

But what if there were a fly in the ointment?

What if changes began to happen in our company: a merger, for example? There could be changes outside the company too, such as the threat posed by a new competitor. Could this mean that our vision for health and safety won't last the distance?

We know that today's companies are facing a lot of change, but the main problem is the speed of that change. The acronym VUCA – first used in 1987 and based on the leadership theories of Bennis and Nanus[9] – describes the volatility, uncertainty, complexity and ambiguity of general conditions and situations, particularly for businesses. It is enough to test the most resilient of business strategies.

What if, while buffeted by the many storms of change that our companies are likely to face over the next five to 10 years, our vision isn't big enough to stay afloat?

For health and safety, it may well be big enough, but what about all the other important issues that are already vying for our company's attention? From quality to sustainability, diversity and inclusion, there are plenty of new causes competing for attention on the corporate agenda.

Our H&S leadership program is also a behavioral change program, meaning that we need to define the behaviors we want to see for health and safety. With all the other imperatives that our company and our employees will need to take care of, what other behaviors might we need? Will we need a different set of behaviors for each strategic initiative?

Let's get into our time machine and propel ourselves forward – safely of course – five years into the future. Our company now wants to invest in some of these other challenges, and it also requires leadership from all employees to be successful.

We are a few years into our H&S leadership program, and it is going well. Most employees have already adopted the new behaviors, and the H&S culture has improved significantly. Why wouldn't we then extend our program and our leadership behaviors to other parts of the business?

Of course, this would make sense, but we can only do this if we have already considered it at the design phase. Otherwise, we will end up with a set of leadership behaviors that really work only for health and safety and can't be applied elsewhere, no matter how hard we try.

Other strategic initiatives will require a new and additional set of employee behaviors, and employees won't be happy about this. After all, who wants to have to change their behavior every time their company decides to focus on something different? Aren't there some common factors in the success of everything we do at work?

What we need to do is to consider the possibility of extending our program's behaviors into other areas, at the design phase. This doesn't mean ending up with a set of behaviors so generic and wishy washy that they don't end up working for health and safety. But it does mean considering slight tweaks at the design phase to give us more flexibility later. These tweaks may be required for all parts of the program, not just the behaviors.

So here we go; let's design our H&S leadership behaviors and while we are doing it, let's make sure that they last the distance.

We need to start by making sure that they are evidence based. We need to analyze *all our H&S incidents* for safe and unsafe, healthy and unhealthy, behaviors. What behaviors do we see as the root cause of most of our incidents? Let's group them into themes and think about which behaviors would need to be in place to prevent those incidents happening again.

It is all in the data

Andi was in the management team and had been tasked with getting the company focused on health and safety. It had some great systems and lots of rules in place, but there were still H&S issues. Two-thirds of these were down to behaviors, unsafe actions or human error. Andi thought about putting in place some behaviors for employees to follow, behaviors that would increase the likelihood of everyone staying safe and well. But what would they look like? Behaviors could be so subjective. Then Andi had a brainwave.

Surely all he had to do was to find out which behaviors (or lack thereof) were most commonly at the root of the most serious incidents, and then communicate the need to adopt their safe equivalent. So that is what he did. He asked the H&S team to trawl through the incident data in detail, looking for the behavioral commonalities. The results were revealing, giving him seven H&S behaviors for the company to adopt. And they were easy to sell to the workforce as well, since everyone knew they were based on past incidents and could help prevent them happening again. Now they finally had an effective health and safety solution.

At the beginning, we may have far more behaviors than we need, but we need to start somewhere. Even at this longlist stage, we need to make sure that our behaviors are expressed in positive terms. Let's say what we *do* want our employees to do, rather than what we *don't* want them to do.

This is because if we use a negative instruction such as "Don't do a job for which you are not trained and competent," or "Don't use cleaning detergents without your protective gloves on," the brain has to read the suggestion in the statement in order to process the negative. This will result in employees taking the suggestion and doing exactly what we asked them not to do.

To check the logic behind this, ask yourself how many times you have forgotten your keys, having told yourself not to forget them? How many times have your children done precisely the thing that you had just asked them not to do?

It is easy to be skeptical until we hear about the work of French pharmacist Emil Coué.[10] He dispensed medicines every day between 1882 and 1910 from a pharmacy in Troyes, France. Every time he handed over a medicine, he spoke highly of its efficacy to the recipient. Over time Coué observed that all his customers seemed to report how well their medicines had worked. This shows that when we believe a medicine will work due to the power of suggestion, our unconscious minds take the suggestion and tell our physical body to make it so.

Coué's observation was what we now call the 'placebo effect.' He became famous for his subsequent work on autosuggestion and for the affirmation "Every day, in every way, I am getting better and better."

Making positive suggestions to our unconscious mind has had incredible effects in the field of healing. It also works brilliantly in the sporting arena. Olympic athletes train hard not only physically, but also mentally, by using positive statements about what they are capable of achieving. As Napoleon Hill, an American self-help author born in 1883 famously said, "What the mind believes, the body can achieve."

As individuals we often feel that we are in control of our actions, but there is a part of our brain which is autonomous, and far more likely to be driving our behavior. Otherwise known as our unconscious mind or our instinctive brain, this part of us responds well to simple and direct suggestion.

So, back to our list of behaviors. Once we have shown this list to our key stakeholders, we can begin the process of whittling them down to a shortlist, which should have no more than seven behaviors. This is important because a study by cognitive psychologist George A. Miller, of Harvard University, published in *Psychological Review* (1956),[11] showed that seven (plus or minus two) was the magic number for people to remember, and beyond which the human brain would struggle.

As we start to finalize our chosen behaviors, we need to remember Coué's work and be clear about what we want to see in our company. We need to make the language short and simple, so that everyone can understand it. During the Covid-19 pandemic, people were instructed to "stay at home." This sounds like a clear instruction, although we could argue that "stay at home" is too generic, and that no one really knew what it meant. We also need to remember to include examples of the behavior, and what it means for different people in different contexts.

Netflix has been lauded in the business world for the quality of its culture. The history of how it was built is described in Erin Meyer's book, *No Rules Rules: Netflix and the Culture of Reinvention* (2020),[12] which was co-written with Netflix's chairman and CEO, Reed Hastings.

When you go to the Netflix website, you will notice that it doesn't just talk about company values, but instead is very clear about what behaviors are expected of its employees, to fulfill its company values.

Example of Netflix Value and Associated Behaviors

(Source www.jobs.netflix.com/culture)

Value: Impact

You accomplish amazing amounts of important work.

You demonstrate consistently strong performance so colleagues can rely upon you.

You make your colleagues better.

You focus on results over process.

We can test our behaviors by looking for examples of how we might use them in different operational contexts, and for different job roles.

Finally, we need to remember that if we want our behaviors, and our H&S movement, to last, our behaviors need to be *adaptable*.

Let's ask ourselves whether our behaviors are generic enough to work for all parts of our business? Will they still work for future strategic issues, other than health and safety? It might mean just a tweak of a word or two, here and there, to give them room to grow.

For example, say you discover that a key issue in your health and safety incidents is that people blindly push ahead with their work, despite issues such as incomplete equipment or instructions, without questioning whether there is a safer way of doing things. Your H&S behavior may therefore be "Ask questions about health and safety" while your more generic behavior could be "Ask questions whenever there is an information gap."

Once we have our list and we are happy that it accurately represents the H&S behaviors that we are looking for, all we need to do now is give them a name.

What should we call our H&S leadership behaviors?

What name do we need to give them, to make sure that our employees:

1. understand them?
2. remember them?
3. adopt them?
4. do all the above with ease?

Your H&S behaviors are ready. Now prepare yourself to forge company-wide partnerships based on win-win propositions, to begin to make "H&S first and owned by all" a reality.

 **Checklist 5**

Nine steps to defining a set of H&S behaviors

1. EVIDENCE. Analyze the issues, problems and incidents underlying each of your strategic issues and look for commonalities. What behaviors do you see as the root cause of each issue?

2. THEMES. Find the behavioral themes in the common issues. What themes exist in those issues and what behaviors, if put into place, would prevent those issues from happening again?

3. LONGLIST. Draft a longlist of required behaviors, based on the themes uncovered in step 2 above.

4. LANGUAGE. Before you go any further, check that each of your behaviors is formulated in the positive. Make sure that you state what the employee is required to do, rather than not to do.

5. SHORTLIST. Group your longlist into common areas and whittle them down to a shortlist of no more than seven.

6. TEST. Test your behavior set with every different operational area of your business, to check that the language makes sense to them.

7. REFINE. Based on the feedback received from operations, change the language of your behaviors to ensure that they make sense to all.

8. ALIGN. Go back again to your key operational contacts and ask for examples of how each of the seven behaviors can be deployed across each of your strategic issues.

9. NAME. Finally, you need a name for your behavior set. Make it short, memorable and meaningful, then promote, promote, promote!

Action focus 5

For senior managers:
Use behaviors as a focus with employees the next time you visit a worksite. Actively look for what you think are safe behaviors and reinforce them by praising them and being specific about the behavior you are praising. When you see unsafe behaviors, let the employee know what you have noticed, and ask them what they need to behave more safely. Make a note of the safe and unsafe behaviors and feed them back to the health and safety team.

For health and safety professionals:
Go through all your serious health and safety incidents over the previous 12 months and identify which behaviors (or lack of) were the likely root cause, and the behaviors that could have prevented them.

For the communications and engagement manager:
Provide your support to the health and safety team in finding language around behaviors that fits all areas of the business.

For the HR director:
Compare the H&S behaviors to any existing leadership behaviors and produce a matrix showing how and where they support each other.

Zoe Hands, chief operating officer

Employees at all levels will tell you that they are too busy to get involved in health and safety. Often it is because they either can't see the relevance to their job role, or because they view health and safety as boring and bureaucratic.

This perception has changed since the Covid-19 pandemic, but it is still up to the leaders of the company, supported by a good H&S function, to encourage employees to get involved. H&S commitment needs to be led from the top, and this requires a regular investment of time. That time must be invested before, not after, something goes wrong.

One of the best strategies, in my experience as a former H&S director, is to clearly define a single set of rules or behaviors that you want to see from all your employees, based on the key H&S risks that exist in the business. Companies and employees have information overload, so we need to keep these rules or behaviors simple and help people to integrate them into their daily activities. This is how we make them a habit, rather than yet another competing priority.

Once defined, your rules or behaviors need to be communicated, and communicated again, to the workforce. They need to be relevant to different work activities and employees must understand why they exist. Your senior leadership team will begin this cascade, so make sure that you meet each of them individually, to emphasize how important it is for them to know, follow and drive the adoption of these behaviors. They also need to take time to understand the individual and company factors behind errors and violations that could undermine them, so that they know how to help avoid these pitfalls.

Finally, these rules or behaviors need to have consequences: positive consequences, so that employees are more likely to repeat the right behavior, and negative consequences for non-compliance. Make sure that you don't just home in on employee behavior, without analyzing the whole system that created the environment for the behavior to happen.

This is where the 'just culture model,' which is a values-supportive model of shared accountability, comes in useful. This allows you to hold people to account for willful violations, but at the same time encourages analysis and learning rather than blame.

Diagram 1 – Building the foundations for
transformational health and safety.

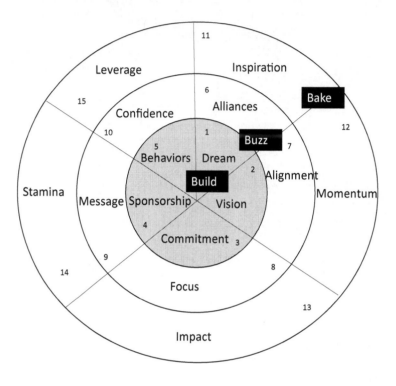

PART 2

BUZZ

CHAPTER 6

Alliances: Forge partnerships across the company

We have dared to believe that health and safety can transform our company. This daring belief comes from a deep-seated value that people come first, even in business, where profit is usually the key driver.

We have also dared to suggest to the rest of our management team that people and profit aren't necessarily two conflicting goals.

We have imagined what success looks like and set an ambitious vision to achieve it.

We have convinced the entire management team that putting health and safety first means putting people first. They now understand that putting people first is the fastest route to improved performance and therefore profit.

We have put the key foundations in place for the vehicle that is going to make all of this happen: our dedicated H&S leadership program, our H&S movement. This includes our H&S leadership behaviors.

Now it is time to take it up a gear and move into Part 2 – BUZZ.

We now need to really bring caring for our employees to life, making this an everyday reality by creating a buzz about it.

This phase is all about making sure that our program is successful. It is where we remind ourselves that an H&S leadership program is, in effect, a cultural change program. We know from experience that unfortunately more cultural change programs fail than succeed. But why is this?

No doubt there are many reasons, and every company is different, but the main barrier to a cultural change program succeeding is people. If enough people in the company decide to resist the change that we are proposing, for whatever reason, then we won't succeed, or our success will be minimal or fleeting.

To avoid this at all costs, we need to take action. Action that will maximize the chances of our new H&S leadership program being a success and ensure that we see a return on our investment. This action requires harnessing the very thing that we just said was the main barrier to our success: people. Because people are also our route to more success than we ever thought possible.

So how do we quantify that success with a topic such as health and safety? How do we measure a return on people staying safe and well?

Ensuring that no one ever gets hurt in our workplaces is the ultimate return, but whether we can see or quantify this or not, will depend on a number of different variables.

Perhaps just knowing that people are less likely to get hurt, or feeling confident that we are doing the right things, is more important.

What we really want to ensure is that our new initiative gets adopted, embedded and acted upon, by all employees, across the entire business, for the long term.

We may think that some of this is out of our hands, but there are steps we can take before we even design our H&S leadership program to maximize its impact.

It is worth remembering here that the people who will adopt our program – our employees – are already busy people. No doubt they are already being asked to work smarter and do more with less. They will adopt something new only if they think that it adds value to the company and, crucially, if it doesn't make their job more difficult.

To do this, we need a program that does the following:

1. Addresses real challenges in the business.
2. Speaks the language of the different workplaces.
3. Streamlines with existing processes.
4. Improves health and safety.
5. Acts as a lever for other business priorities.

When we have achieved all of this, we will get widespread adoption of our H&S leadership program.

First there is some essential work to be done, before our program can launch.

This is because buy-in only comes when people feel involved, so we need to get them involved early on. A program that fits the unique needs of our business can be created only once those unique needs have been examined, understood and designed in from the start.

The more people who have bought into and are adopting our program, the more likely it is that it will pay back its initial investment, in terms of health and safety. This will also make it more likely to have a positive impact on other parts of the business.

So here is what we need to do in the Buzz phase, before we even launch our H&S leadership program.

Engage with our key stakeholders and forge alliances across our company with the people who will champion and drive our program.

Speak to our H&S communities, our management teams and the functions that can help us, including HR, learning and development (L&D), communications and engagement, and training.

These are all business functions that have a stake in our program, even if that stake isn't instantly obvious. We know that this is an H&S leadership program, owned by the H&S function, but it is also a general leadership program. This is an area in which other parts of the business already have expertise, and feel a sense of ownership over, so we need to be sensitive to this fact.

We need to engage with the HR function; by looking at the company's values and behaviors, and how our H&S leadership program behaviors will align and fit with them. The more aligned they are, the happier our HR colleagues will be, and the easier it will be for employees to adopt our H&S leadership program.

The HR function, including L&D and talent management, will be interested in our H&S leadership program. They will want to ensure that it supports, rather than contradicts, the company's existing values, behaviors and culture. During the Covid-19 pandemic, the HR and H&S functions worked more closely together than ever before, coordinating their responses to look after employees and paving the way for a long-term partnership.

Our H&S leadership program is also a large-scale exercise in employee communications and engagement, so early engagement with the communications team is essential. We need not only to get them on board, but also to fully understand the essence of our program. After all, if they don't get it, how can they possibly communicate it?

Don't be a flash in the pan

Michelle had been brought into the company specifically to deliver an H&S leadership program, and her boss was eager to see results. Michelle had explained that this was a long-term endeavor, and that he and the rest of the management team needed to be patient, but he was still urging her to launch the program as soon as possible. Michelle knew that while she may get some kudos from her boss for getting a program like this out quickly, she would get much more praise over the long term if it didn't end up being just a 'flash in the pan.'

She was also pretty much on her own in terms of resources, so she needed allies across the business who could lend their support. From the beginning, Michelle invested her time in building relationships around the business and selling her ideas to everyone who would listen. This strategy paid off because once her program launched, not only was it the right one, but it took off more quickly than everyone had expected. And amid the long-term focus, she still managed to find a quick win when one employee used his learning from the program to prevent what could have been a nasty accident.

We may consider running some taster sessions for our program, even it is only in the early development stages. That way our important key stakeholders will be able to experience what we intend to offer, before anyone else in the business. This will mean that they understand its key selling points and, importantly, that they will be able to offer feedback on how it might be received by employees.

We also need to remember to engage our company's training function. Again, this might be our H&S leadership program, but it is likely to contain a large training element, and we probably already have training experts in our company.

Admittedly, an H&S leadership program is not your average training program. While most training is designed to impart knowledge and improve skills; our training is intended to change behaviors. This means it needs to be designed and delivered differently.

Our training colleagues will still be invaluable allies, however, as they know how to plan and deliver training successfully in a large company. They already have all the training processes set up, and we will need their valuable support, and maybe even some of their trainers. When rolling out a program using internal trainers, as we shall with this program, we shall also need a robust 'train the trainer' process to support it.

All the key stakeholders we mention above are an important sounding board at this early stage, and hence critical to our success.

They are also the people who have influence over others and who are most likely to champion our program. Who knows, they may even lend us resources and partner with us to help us succeed; now that would be a good outcome.

By partnering early on with all the functions or managers who have a stake and an interest in our program, we stand a good chance of it being successful in the short term. Having achieved short-term success, our program will also stand a better chance of becoming integrated into the company over the long term. It is this integration which is key to our overall success.

Once our program and its behaviors are integrated, they will become difficult to ignore. Our aim is to get our H&S leadership program as embedded as possible into the processes on which our company relies.

Many H&S professionals forget the importance of embedding, in the heady build-up to launching something as exciting as an H&S leadership program.

Equally important at this stage is engaging with the operational side of our business – with the workers who are most at risk and who act as our last line of defense. In a large company, we may have many different population types, doing different types of work in different places, and we will need to make sure that our program speaks their language. In a smaller company, we just need to engage all the managers.

We will also want some of our operational people to champion our program and sign up to become trainers.

This is why we need to reach out to our heads of department, holding one-to-one conversations with them about our intentions, and asking permission to pilot our program with a sample audience from their area.

Nothing is off limits at this early stage. We should be holding focus groups, asking lots of questions, and of course listening to the answers.

This information gathering is going to be invaluable in guiding our H&S leadership program.

It will enable us to assess the potential barriers to success and the opportunities. This will help us to drive the program forward, at a company, team and individual level.

It is important to ask for success stories, allowing us to build on and leverage what already works in our company's culture, or H&S culture if it already exists.

We need to request opinions, ideas and details about their feelings from individuals throughout our company, for example:

- What is their idea of an H&S leadership program?

- How do they feel about H&S leadership in the company?

- What would *they* do to make it a success?

- What would make *them* want to be involved?

This final question "What would make them want to be involved?" will help us to "think win-win." This is Stephen Covey's fourth habit from his book (1989), which we talked about at the start of Chapter 2. This is about seeking mutual benefit from all human interactions, instead of having winners on one side and losers on the other.

If our partnerships with others in the company are based on *both* parties benefiting in some way, not just us, they are more likely to prosper. The longer these partnerships last, the longer our H&S leadership program will last.

The more of this mutual benefit we can get up front, the more information we will have to guide our program design.

Interviewing our key stakeholders also demonstrates that we have consulted with and listened to them. This will make it more likely that they will lead our program when we need them to.

Ultimately, our H&S leadership program is an exercise in influence and persuasion. Its impact will depend on the strength of our networks and communities, and the degree to which they trust us.

It is never too early to build that trust, because when employees trust, they become confident H&S leaders.

H&S leadership is all about engagement, but the most important part is the engagement that takes place before the formal engagement begins. We are clearly talking about 'pre-engagement engagement' here, which is not an official term but is an important concept nevertheless.

It is important to take as much time as we need to build up the right relationships before we even think about launching our H&S leadership program.

Make sure that you have invested properly in building cross-company alliances for health and safety. In the next chapter, we are going to check that our program design has no gaps.

⏻ Checklist 6

How to forge alliances across the company

1. Write a list of all departments or functions that have a stake in your program, for example, HR, L&D, communications and training.

2. Write an inventory of all existing procedures and content that your program needs to align with to be successful, for example, company values and existing leadership behaviors, training and HR processes.

3. Decide on the win-win – what will your program offer these people and what will they offer your program? What is the common goal?

4. Engage with all these stakeholders early, before your program launches.

5. Give your stakeholders an opportunity to get involved in co-creating and designing some of the program's content.

6. Put a plan together for how you will work with all these departments, for example, a communications plan to launch the program.

7. Identify your key operational stakeholders, making sure you have one from each different business unit, covering all your business activities.

8. Make early contact with your operational stakeholders to explain what your program will do for them.

9. Pilot your program with each different operational team.

10. Use their feedback to customize your program's content and language.

 Action focus 6

For senior managers:
How can you encourage and recognize cross-company collaboration for health and safety?

For health and safety professionals:
Draw up a win-win chart that compares what your health and safety program needs against the needs of other key stakeholders.

For the communications and engagement manager:
What are the benefits for the communications function of getting involved in health and safety engagement?

For the HR director:
What are the benefits for the HR function of getting involved in health and safety leadership?

Sarah Kerr, head of health and safety

The role of health and safety in business is to ensure that work colleagues and our customers alike get home safely to their loved ones every day. Human relationships are the starting point for everything we do, and in a very technical discipline, it is easy for this to be forgotten, especially by those who see H&S teams as simply rule enforcers. This is why it is crucial for companies to support their H&S teams to take time to create and develop relationships across the company. Essentially, it's about trust. We know that while trust can be broken in a heartbeat, it often takes years to build. H&S leadership is the same, needing time to build the right relationships with employees and key internal stakeholders.

Of course not everyone in the company realizes the relevance of health and safety to them and their job role, especially if they are in a non-operational or office role. It is up to H&S teams to make that relevance clear and to show how employee health and safety is impacted by the decisions and actions made and taken by other parts of the business and can be boosted by them.

This is why successful H&S leadership programs aren't delivered solely by an H&S team but in collaboration with various stakeholders across the organization. The secret is to bring meaning to the H&S story by connecting it to the company story as a whole, with its vision, values and behaviors. This is the golden thread that brings everyone together: health and safety at the center of everything the company is trying to do, rather than a costly add-on required only for external compliance.

The best starting point is to assume that all stakeholders in the business have a different perception of what health and safety is, and that this varies depending on their specific agenda. When companies can show the value of health and safety to the company as a whole, and create win-win partnerships across the business, everyone becomes advocates of the H&S agenda.

This is why technical health and safety, while critical in companies, is not all there is to this important topic. The way to make it relevant to others is to focus on what unites us all, rather than what divides us, with that common denominator being the human side. The health and safety message needs to be predominantly about caring, and the starting point for this is listening to employees, finding out about their hopes, dreams and challenges, and their views of health and safety.

Storytelling is key, and when you can share stories about health and safety across the business, and encourage others to do the same, the topic will resonate with everyone. I have heard many a true story about health and safety, and the impact of workplace accidents, told in H&S training sessions. These have converted even the biggest skeptics. Don't rely just on metrics to measure the success of the training; the best metrics are the stories people will tell you about how they felt as a result of it. Bring caring into health and safety and the engagement will take care of itself. It may even extend to your customers.

CHAPTER 7

Alignment: Plan your H&S movement

We have already done most of the hard work to design our H&S program. We have H&S champions in all the right places, and we have built alliances across the company. All senior stakeholders are on board, our program is ready to launch and our network is poised and ready.

Now is a good time therefore to remind ourselves what we want to achieve.

Our goal is to create a culture where everyone, not just the H&S function, owns health and safety. When this happens, we will have not only an H&S function in the company, but an H&S movement.

When everyone owns health and safety, it creates a culture that provides a strong foundation for the reduction of H&S incidents. In this culture, every employee takes responsibility for following our rules and procedures and will politely call out those who don't. All of this increases the likelihood, and our confidence, that employees will go home every day safe and free from harm and feel more engaged and motivated generally.

It sounds simple, and it is in theory, but putting this into practice is much harder. There are two main reasons for this:

1. Many employees don't see the relevance of health and safety to them. They don't see the risks to them in the workplace, and they believe that having an H&S function or an H&S manager means that any risks have already been taken care of.

2. The global nature of today's companies, regardless of size, often makes it difficult to reach every single employee, particularly those in far-flung corners of the world, to get the health and safety message through to them.

When designing your H&S culture, it helps to keep these barriers in mind, remembering how people think, and what it takes to motivate them. Employees will only take ownership of health and safety when they are personally motivated to do so.

The word 'motivation' can make us think about the carrot and stick approach, that is, using rewards (carrots) and punishments (sticks) to induce desired behaviors. This approach certainly gets results, at least in the short term. Human beings will quickly adopt new behaviors when they perceive that there is a significant risk, or when a big enough reward is dangled in front of them.

Sometimes, however, this approach can be counterproductive, if managers find themselves chasing impressive numbers, while forgetting what they are really trying to achieve. It is great that employees are motivated to spot safety hazards and threats to mental and physical health, for example, but what if the incoming data is submitted just to achieve a target? As we busy ourselves creating our movement, we need to make sure that we are motivating our employees to focus on the right things and not getting overzealous with the carrot.

Carrot and stick type motivation mechanisms also fizzle out when other mechanisms take priority. We humans can be fickle at times and our attention is easily diverted. One carrot might interest us today, but may not tempt us tomorrow, and being metaphorically beaten with a stick is hardly the best motivator in the workplace.

In the long term, employees' motivation for one initiative will quickly wane in favor of the next one. So what is the solution?

In his groundbreaking book, *Drive: The Surprising Truth About What Motivates Us* (2009),[13] Daniel Pink says the solution is 'Motivation 3.0,' consisting of three key elements of 'Intrinsic Motivation,' which are **autonomy**, **mastery** and **purpose**. This definitely applies to our H&S mission, especially if we look at these in reverse order.

We have already given our employees a sense of **purpose** through our ALTE vision back in Chapter 2.

Now we need to consider how we allow them to excel at, or become **masters** of, their role as H&S leaders.

We also need to ensure that they have **autonomy** over how they do it.

These three motivational factors ensure that people remain motivated over the long term in a sustainable way.

Daniel Pink's Theory of Motivation

Motivation 1.0: Primitive Survival

Motivation 2.0: Extrinsic Motivation

Type X: Carrots and sticks/reward and punishment – short term, can backfire.

Motivation 3.0: Intrinsic Motivation

Type I: Autonomy, mastery, purpose – long-term, sustainable

There are six other elements that we also need to consider. These are values, vision, identity, beliefs, skills and behaviors. Let's take a closer look at the impact these can have.

To sustain the new behaviors, we need to engage employees emotionally around health and safety, so that it becomes something they feel so passionately about, they do it without even thinking. To do this we need to reach their deep motivational drivers: the things that don't change daily. These are our personal **values** and are sometimes so deep-seated that our conscious brain is not even aware of them. They still impact our behavior though, so they can't be ignored.

Every single employee in our company is different, with different values, but our employees *can* all become aligned around one thing. We have already set an ambitious H&S **vision** and done our utmost to make sure that this will be a vision that everyone can feel excited to be part of.

Have you heard the story about the janitor working for NASA who in 1961 was asked by the president of the United States,

John F. Kennedy, what his role was in the company? The janitor responded, "I'm helping put a man on the moon." It is fair to say that this man was pretty engaged with NASA's vision. He knew that he was following a purpose bigger than himself. The goal was clear to him, and he felt part of it.

So, do *we* need to give all employees an **identity** they can be proud of when it comes to health and safety? We have said that we need everyone to be leaders for health and safety, but do they know this? Have we told them that everyone is an H&S leader, regardless of their role or position in the company? Have we made everyone feel empowered?

We said earlier that values are key drivers of behavior, so we need to make this an integral part of the design of our H&S movement. It is not enough to tell people that health and safety is a value for the company: we have to make it meaningful, by communicating differently.

Using logical arguments for why people should behave in a healthy and safe manner is important, but as we said in Chapter 2, where we talked about having a vision, human beings make decisions based on emotions as well. We can awaken those emotions with stories, metaphors and experiences, which will allow us to communicate in a way that has personal meaning.

All values have beliefs associated with them. Beliefs are our rules for life and tell us how to behave. We cannot address H&S behaviors without looking at the **beliefs** our employees need to hold if they are to be successful in putting health and safety first. As Henry Ford once said, "If you think you can or think you can't – you're right."

If employees believe they can make a difference for health and safety, by behaving in a certain way, then they will change their behavior, but if they don't believe it will matter, they won't. It all starts with belief.

Vision, identity, values and beliefs are critical, but not enough by themselves. We also need to give our employees the **skills** to feel confident in their new identity as H&S leaders. We need to give them leadership skills so that they feel able to speak out with sensitivity and confidence, challenging and coaching others to keep their colleagues healthy and safe.

All this needs to be considered and planned in advance if we are to turn our H&S program into a movement.

There is one final element to consider and that is **behaviors.** We have already defined what we want to see in an H&S leader. In effect, these behaviors give us our blueprint for H&S leadership in *our* company. I emphasize *our* company because we have defined the behaviors based on an understanding of our own H&S incidents.

To bring these behaviors to life in our movement, we need to take the extra step of explaining how they vary, at different levels of the company, and link them to overall performance objectives.

Are you in?

A few years ago, a manufacturing company wanted to get a competitive edge over everyone else in their industry. After consulting a team of behavioral psychologists, the management team came up with an elevator pitch to achieve this goal. They decided to leverage the 'health and safety first' message as their strategy to get ahead. At their quarterly 'town hall' meeting, shortly after this decision was made, the CEO stood in front of 900 employees, which was almost the whole company, and said:

> Colleagues, I want our company to be the most caring company in our industry. No one should ever get hurt

or sick as a result of working here. But I am going to need your help. I am going to need every single one of you to get involved, to make my vision a reality. If your health and safety, and that of your colleagues, is as important to you as it is to me, then please play your part, and become an H&S leader. I believe that every H&S accident or incident can and will be prevented, as long as we act together. If you believe this too, get on board! Attend the training we are offering you in H&S leadership and communication, take the behaviors we need from you to heart, and make them part of your daily habits. Your lives, and those of your colleagues, depend on it. Are you in?

Over the next five years, employees at the company were instrumental in improving the H&S culture.

These six topics, and the questions they raise, are the key elements of our H&S movement. They build alignment for a one-company approach. They also build alignment within employees themselves because they address the key drivers of our behavior.

Even once our program has launched, we can use them to keep an eye on it, making adjustments, if necessary, to ensure that it continues to provide the impact, and the ownership, that we are seeking.

These six topics also provide an excellent framework for our elevator pitch, giving us a framework to describe our movement to others.

Armed with the six key elements of our H&S movement, we now need to turn our attention to our H&S people.

These are the people who will get our movement started. But do they have the right focus?

⏻ Checklist 7

The key elements of an H&S leadership movement

1. Create a vision or a purpose for your H&S mission.

2. Create an identity for the mission that all employees can buy into: for example, everyone is an H&S leader, regardless of their job role.

3. Ensure that health and safety is a personal value for all, and a non-negotiable priority, no matter what the circumstances.

4. Define the beliefs employees need to hold about health and safety, in order to make the vision a reality.

5. Identify the skills and capabilities employees need to have, to fulfill their identity as defined in point 2 above.

6. Define the behaviors that employees need to adopt to make the vision a reality.

 Action focus 7

For senior managers:
Learn the elevator pitch for health and safety produced by the communications team and find ways to incorporate it into your daily conversations.

For health and safety professionals:
Draw up a diagram showing the six elements of alignment for an H&S movement, and what they mean for your company.

For the communications and engagement manager:
Create a company-wide message for health and safety based on the six-point alignment diagram created by health and safety. Create three versions – short article, 30-second elevator pitch and six words only. Consider any adaptations for different job roles, levels and worksites.

For the HR director:
Consider how the six-point alignment diagram fits with any other company-wide leadership initiative.

Benjamin Legg, corporate health and safety director

In my view, health and safety has an image problem and yet it is such a valuable and enabling topic. Why is this? Across industry and society, I believe our subject matter is not always embraced or indeed fully understood. Part of the problem is inherent in what we do, but part of it is self-created, and reflects how we relate to colleagues, customers, industry and business through the language we use and how we engage. These issues need to be addressed if we are to truly inspire an organization to embrace and enable focus on health and safety, to the extent that it becomes an exciting corporate movement.

For us to continue to improve health and safety in companies, and to turn a topic that is perceived to be dry and pessimistic into a positive force for change, we have a number of challenges to consider. When we start by confronting them head on, these challenges can be surmounted and even turned into an opportunity. Yes, we can deliver safer, more engaged, more resilient and more psychologically safe workplaces, and in a more consistent and constant fashion. One of the biggest challenges we face is how we make the health and safety function relevant in our companies, and truly integrate it within them.

The problem starts with health and safety sometimes being perceived as a barrier to business and production – a source of problems fueled from the audits and inspections we conduct. What we need instead is to be valued for our ability to enable change and improvement, and to act as a catalyst for enhanced delivery and heightened risk and opportunity management.

In most businesses, health and safety is seen as a reactive function that is called upon when things go wrong. I believe that we need to lead more proactively on doing the right things for health and safety. That way, we will engage our people and prevent incidents and accidents before they occur. Our function is ideally positioned to drive increased engagement and better working environments, and to be a source of innovation.

The first step is to understand our internal customers, and how health and safety can support and integrate with enhanced business delivery. This means shifting our mindset from compliance to ownership and striving to get closer to our non-H&S colleagues, utilizing a language that is collaborative and dare I say simple.

I believe that we have an opportunity as a function to lead a culture that supports active involvement and innovation in health and safety. One where people feel safe enough to admit to mistakes, which can then be discussed openly and learned from. We need to make health and safety less complex and more accessible to our colleagues and inspire them to get involved.

When all of this happens, health and safety will become a movement, because the entire company will be focused on it, and we will all benefit. From the CEO to managers, from supervisors to employees, and even the public at large, it is to all our benefit to keep health and safety front and center, integrated and relevant. Never has this been more evident than during the Covid-19 pandemic.

CHAPTER 8

Focus: Get your H&S teams ready

We have done our early homework, put the foundations in place and reached out to key stakeholders. Our H&S movement has been sketched out, and it is time to get our H&S people involved.

The H&S people in our company must naturally be the ones to take ownership of our new H&S leadership approach, right? The truth is they may not be. Certainly, they will have the subject matter expertise for health and safety, but they won't necessarily have the people skills required to deliver this kind of transformational change. At the very least they may need to change their focus to deliver the message in the right way.

If our H&S program is going to be successful and become a movement, it will need to deliver an H&S message that is completely different from the messages that have been communicated before. It will also need to be delivered in a completely different way.

As Henry Ford said, "If you always do what you always did, you'll always get what you always got."

For the challenge ahead of us, this is certainly true.

To turn health and safety into a movement, we can't simply *do* health and safety as we did before, or we will just get the same result we have always had.

The good news is that we have probably already achieved a high level of compliance in our company, especially since Covid-19, and this is a good place to start. It provides us with a great springboard to move beyond compliance and take our H&S culture to the next level. We want to achieve levels of compliance that come only from increased levels of engagement around health and safety.

So yes, health and safety is about compliance, but it is also about ownership through engagement, and the only thing that will drive more compliance is more ownership. This is where we can apply Daniel Pink's Motivation 3.0 model of autonomy, mastery and purpose, which we looked at in Chapter 7.

We want our employees to be engaged around health and safety, motivated in the three ways we mention above, that is, connected to a higher purpose; wanting to achieve excellence; and having the autonomy to do get on with it. This will then lead to our employees actively seeking more health and safety knowledge and challenging the company to do more itself.

Our aim is total engagement around health and safety, so much so that employees want to take ownership of H&S systems, processes, rules and procedures.

This leads us on to two key questions:

1. How aware are your H&S people of our aim of total engagement?

2. How capable do they feel of achieving it?

As we know, H&S professionals are extremely well trained in technical skills, and that is why they are experts in what they do. They spend years studying their trade and are well versed in the complex H&S legislation that protects both companies and workers.

H&S professionals are equally well versed in methods and procedures. They know the correct methods of working to keep people healthy and safe, and they dedicate their working lives to making sure that other people follow these methods. If you are reading this book having never been involved in an H&S incident, then it is probably not down to luck, but thanks to the hard work of your H&S person or people, or perhaps yourself.

During the Covid-19 pandemic, companies relied more than ever before on their H&S teams, as they moved swiftly to put additional and ever-changing H&S protocols in place. Health and safety became the central information point for everything, and our H&S managers became the new heroes of our companies.

This focus on compliance demands a particular type of language, the language of possibility, where we talk about what *needs*, *must* and *has to* be done. For example, "We *need* to have a proper traffic management system in place," or "We *must* make sure that our risk assessments are up to date."

To achieve engagement and ownership, our language needs to change from necessity to possibility. We want to talk about what *could* be done rather than what *should* be done. So instead of *needing* to make sure that we have a proper traffic management system in place, we could instead ask *"What are the options* for protecting our people, by segregating them from vehicles?"*

This subtle shift in language makes a big difference to the receiver, because being asked to consider options and choices, rather than duties and obligations, is a lot more empowering than simply being told what to do. It is also more engaging to hear this language because having choices is always more attractive.

Feeling engaged and empowered around health and safety is likely to lead to employees getting more involved in health and safety. More importantly, they are more likely to choose to take ownership of it in their work area or department, which will help to prevent incidents and illnesses as a natural consequence.

In her book, *Words that Change Minds: The 14 patterns for mastering the language of influence* (2019),[14] Shelle Rose Charvet calls this a person's "motivation reason." She theorizes that some people are motivated by following procedures and therefore use this type of language, whereas others are more motivated by the opportunity to break with the status quo and do things differently, which requires a very different way of speaking.

This explains why, if our H&S leadership program is to be a success, we will need its advocates to be talking about breaking with the status quo, regardless of their motivation reason. If we want them to do things differently and adopt new behaviors, then it follows that we need to talk to them differently; we need to inspire and motivate them with our words.

The word that gets heard

When Tom did the rounds for health and safety at his company, checking that people were following the rules; it was the same old story. He would see employees not keeping to the pedestrian walkways, driving too fast around the car park, entering an office without a face covering, or using a stepladder to fix a ceiling tile without three points of contact. For Tom, whose job it was to raise these issues, it was always the same old routine, so well-worn he could almost recite it in his sleep. He would always ask the offender why they weren't following the rules, and why they hadn't considered the risk. The same old excuses came back to him time after time, answers such as, "We've always done it this way," or "It's the only way I can get the job done," or "I was late for a meeting."

Then one day Tom decided to try changing his own approach. Instead of arguing back when an engineer said, "We've always done it this way," Tom found himself asking, "What would happen if we *didn't* always do it this way?" The look on the engineer's face was quite a picture, almost as though he were imagining new possibilities. He was being given the power to make a change himself. Seeing his look of wonder, Tom thought he wouldn't be at all surprised if the engineer started behaving safely from now on. Perhaps Tom would never need to argue back again, now that he had discovered a new way of inspiring and motivating with his words, rather than insisting on compliance.

One month later, Tom was doing his usual rounds and was stopped by that same engineer. "Come and look at this," said the engineer, "if you've got a moment." "Sure," said Tom and followed the engineer to the workshop. What he saw left him flabbergasted – in a good way. The engineer had covered the whiteboard on the wall with his ideas for designing safety into all workshop activities.

While health and safety is a lot about compliance, there is also another, possibly even more critical, element of *ownership*. We can have all the H&S systems and processes in the world in our companies, but it is only people, and their ownership of these systems and processes, that bring them to life.

This all sounds very simple. When we want compliance, we talk about necessity, and when we want ownership, we talk about possibility, but this doesn't always trip off the tongue. This is because the language we use is related to the programs we run in our brains. These are based on our experiences, values, beliefs and many other things, which are unique and personal to us. The language we use results from the habitual running of these programs in our heads, and thus it is very hard to change.

This is why H&S professionals will often be out of their comfort zone when moving into H&S leadership territory because their language will need to change to achieve the results that they want.

Today's H&S professionals need to learn how to flex their language – from necessity to possibility and back again – daily. When we teach H&S leadership, as part of our H&S leadership program, we can choose (spot that language of possibility here) to adopt an approach that will capture hearts and minds.

To do this we must make sure that every H&S person involved in the delivery of our H&S leadership program has been trained in the art of transformational communication. This is a skill that they can use to complement their valuable technical skills.

When the H&S professionals are focused on ownership, ownership is what they will achieve. It is all about transformational communication, and we will look further into how to maximize this in the next chapter.

⏻ Checklist 8

How to prepare H&S people to lead your movement

1. Identify your H&S community.

2. Create an inventory of their skills and capabilities.

3. Define the need for training in leadership, communication and behavioral change.

4. Plan a boot camp with your H&S professionals to meet this training need.

5. Create an online forum for your H&S community to support them and encourage social learning.

6. Establish a focus group to work on program content.

7. Use the above steps to identify those with the ability to lead your program; these are your 'super trainers.'

 Action focus 8

For senior managers:
Commit resources to allow your H&S teams to be upskilled in transformational communication.

For health and safety professionals:
Start a word journal. Keep it in your pocket or bag and start noting down every time you use language of necessity.

For the communications and engagement manager:
Set up an online forum to enable the H&S community to share thoughts and ideas about the new H&S program or approach.

For the HR director:
Look to see if there are any internal training resources to support excellence in communication and workshop facilitation for behavioral change.

Kirsty Mac, executive coach, leadership consultant and speaker

When I think about how to create more ownership of health and safety, I think first as a human being. Health and safety processes may be bought into quickly by some, if there is a chance alignment with their values, but this buy-in may be only fleeting, and others may be more difficult to convince. When we use the words 'bought into,' it suggests that something has been 'sold' to the employee, and when we buy anything, we often lose interest over time. This is why as a leadership specialist, I prefer the words 'build-in' than 'buy-in.' Creating 'build-in' is what H&S professionals need to consider.

Start with **storytelling**, because the stories we tell are the part of our communication that create the meaning for people. We need the visceral stories, drawn from emotion rather than logic, like the one we automatically construct from the following six-word novel that is often attributed to Ernest Hemingway: For sale. Baby shoes. Never worn. Try hearing these six words without creating the story around it and feeling the emotion. What six words might an H&S professional use to tell the story of someone whose life was changed through an accident at work that could have been prevented?

Second, we need **curiosity**. Human beings are naturally curious. We constantly strive to find meaning in what we do. The Covid-19 pandemic shifted our priorities dramatically and led us to create new meaning out of our challenges. Health, safety, and wellness came to the fore, and we created meaning in the new health and safety rules. If we can be curious enough to find out how others make meaning in their lives and why they do what they do, then linking H&S to their hearts *and* their minds becomes so much easier.

Third, we need to **create meaningful connections** with those we wish to influence. In so many sectors now we rely on influencers, and health and safety is no exception. In fact, since Covid-19, H&S professionals not only influence their sector, but the whole of their company. Through influencing key decision-makers, we create cultural ambassadors who influence those around them, thereby spreading the ownership. There are H&S professionals who impress, and those who connect. The latter are the ones we remember.

Finally, H&S professionals need to **listen more**. We create more ownership when we talk less. When we are generous with our listening, we automatically create an environment of support, collaboration and conversation. Ultimately, people getting built into health and safety requires health and safety teams to be upskilled to embrace paradox – how to achieve compliance while at the same time addressing all the human elements that create ownership? And this requires a mindset shift!

Diagram 2 – Balancing compliance AND ownership.

CHAPTER 9

Message: Change the way you communicate forever

Communication is a big part of any transformation program. Arguably it is the only thing that matters. It is certainly the one thing that can make a huge difference to our outcome. No volume of planning and preparation can make up for a program that doesn't have communication at its heart. Furthermore, it needs to be transformational communication spoken by a transformational leader.

Transformational leadership is important for H&S leadership. We know this because research by Barling, Loughlin and Kelloway

(2002)[15] showed that it clearly improves H&S culture and, as a result, H&S performance.

It will be useful therefore to define 'transformational leadership.' Then compare it to its more easily recognized counterpart 'transactional leadership.'

Transactional leadership focuses on results, with management expectations of their employees being simply transactional. The 'transaction' is the delivery of a specific amount of work for a specific reward. This type of leadership works well in certain contexts, for example, in high-pressure situations such as the military, where deadlines are tight, or someone is at risk.

With transactional leadership, communication is clear, authoritative and direct.

Transformational leadership, as its name suggests, aims to transform employee relations, rather than transact with them. This type of leadership transforms the way the recipient thinks about the subject in question.

James McGregor Burns was the first person to talk about transformational leadership, in his book, *Leadership* (1978).[16] It is still today considered to be something of a Holy Grail in companies. He defined this style of leadership as a process whereby "leaders and their followers raise one another to higher levels of morality and motivation." This is exactly what we need to transform our company through health and safety.

To achieve our goals, managers need to lead in a way that brings out the best in every individual, and in groups too. They need to lead in a way that allows individuals and groups to fulfill, and even go beyond, their expected potential.

Transformational leaders have to communicate in a different way. They act more as coaches than as managers. Where a manager gives instructions, a coach explains an idea or a concept, and then asks their team what they think. With a manager, the communication is more top-down, whereas with the coach, the communication is more bottom-up.

Transformational leadership, and the transformational communication it brings about, have the power to change our behaviors.

When we can change our H&S behaviors, we have the potential to save lives and enhance health outcomes.

Existing behaviors are often deeply embedded and unfortunately hard to change. Indeed, if they have become habits, they are often displayed without the person even being aware of it. There is likely to be a degree of emotional attachment to the behavior too.

Both factors make it even more difficult to change behaviors. It *can* be done, however, with the right communication and an understanding of how habits work.

Charles Duhigg wrote a great book about this subject, *The Power of Habit: Why We Do What We Do in Life and Business* (2012),[17] in which he tells us the secrets of how to change our habits for the better. He explains that every behavior is preceded by a trigger and followed by a reward. He suggests that to change the behavior, we need to understand what triggers it and what reward it gives us. In this way we can make sure that the new behavior gives the same mental reward. Otherwise, we will be fighting a losing battle.

In *Nudge* (2009),[18] Thaler and Sunstein also talked about habits and how to change them. They believe that one of the key barriers to forming better habits and behaviors is temptation. They said:

"Self-control problems can be illuminated by thinking about an individual as containing two semiautonomous selves, a far-sighted 'Planner' and a myopic 'Doer.'" The planner is rational, like Mr. Spock from the TV series *Star Trek*, trying to promote our long-term welfare and do what is best for us. The doer is more like Homer Simpson, from the TV series *The Simpsons*, who gives in to temptation and thereby thwarts our best efforts.

Understanding how the mind and our habits work is a great starting point for learning how to communicate behavioral change. Armed with this knowledge, here are seven (there's that magic number again) key things to keep in mind when communicating the importance of adopting certain H&S behaviors to our employees:

1. **Explain the benefits.** When we do this, we start to create trust and opportunity. The person we are communicating with realizes why the behavior is so important, and what is in it for them. When we know why we are being asking to do something, and the benefit to us, it helps enormously. For example, during the Covid-19 pandemic, we understood that not getting infected with the virus ourselves also meant not infecting others, and therefore made us part of a far bigger effort to save lives. Given this knowledge, people were far more willing to change their behavior. Until we truly understand the benefits, it isn't always easy for us to agree to difficult action.

2. **Bring emotion into the message.** As we mentioned earlier in the book, while the human brain does respond to logic, it doesn't respond *only* to logic. It also responds to emotion and often makes decisions based on emotion too. Think about the last time you decided to do something, perhaps donate to a charity, was it a purely logical decision? When we tell the human stories around

why we need the change we are asking for, this brings the emotional element of the new behavior sharply into focus. We then have the motivation to either adopt it for the first time or to keep it going if we were already doing it.

3. **Model the behavior yourself.** We cannot possibly expect anyone to adopt behavior that we don't model ourselves. That is why, for example, anyone in authority needed to be at home when filming their "Stay at home" message during the pandemic. Any other action would have been perceived as hypocritical. Behavioral change needs the involvement of everyone to make a big difference, and this can happen only when it is led from the top. Show others that you are committed to the cause and be sure to make this visible. This is an important part of the transformational leadership approach we advocated earlier. Transformational leadership always starts with self.

4. **Challenge others on their non-compliance.** There are always early adopters of a new behavior, while others are slower to realize its importance, for whatever reason. Peer pressure helps, so if we can politely challenge others to adopt our new behavior, not by telling them off, but by asking them what the right thing to do is, then it will likely get good results. In John Kotter's book, *Our Iceberg Is Melting* (2017), which we mentioned in Chapter 2, the penguins asked the 'Professor' penguin to challenge 'NoNo,' the penguin who always found a reason to challenge the new vision. In the story, the Professor didn't tell NoNo off, but simply questioned his thinking, until NoNo gave up his negative behavior of his own accord.

5. **Know how habits work.** Since old behaviors are habits, and habits are sometimes hard to break, we need to encourage the new behaviors by accepting how the old ones work. For example, when we were out and about, before the

pandemic, we were used to passing close to other people, without a second thought. The trigger for this behavior is 'being in a hurry,' and the result is 'getting from A to B as quickly as possible' with whatever reward that gives us. If we want people to keep a safe distance from others, then we need to recognize that people are rewarding their habits with getting to places more quickly, and therefore we need to make it easier for them to still get the same reward. In a supermarket, for example, this could mean rearranging the traffic flow, so that people can do their shopping quickly *and* at a safe distance from others. Not easy I know, but this is the best way to make new habits work. This is also why people often say, "Change the environment, change the behavior." A simple change to the environment can allow new habits to be adopted quickly.

6. **Be constant.** With the constant bombardment from different communication channels and fake news, we are losing our ability to concentrate, and our trust in who and what to follow. When people are being asked to make a big effort to change their behavior, we need to be consistent, persistent, honest and constant in our communication. Repetition of the message, news on progress towards the end goal, and admission of mistakes and learnings along the way, all instill belief and trust. In fact, there is nothing more inspiring than a manager or a senior leader in a company admitting that they are human and have made a mistake.

7. **Be transformational.** As discussed earlier, behavioral change requires transformational rather than transactional communication. This means speaking in the language of ownership rather than compliance. We do want compliance, of course, but only in a sustainable way. This means we need to get people to take ownership and change their behavior because they want to. This in turn

means asking not telling, letting people know that they have a choice, encouraging the right choices, and inspiring them with a vision of what can be achieved when everyone works together.

It is all about the story

James had launched his H&S leadership program and he wanted a member of the management team to speak at the beginning of every single session, to open it and by doing so make it clear to the participants how important the topic was. James was sure that this was a *genius* idea, but what was he going to get them to say? How could he ensure that their presence at these sessions would make an impact, and their words too?

James thought about what had inspired him to get involved in health and safety. He remembered the time one of his co-workers had told him a story about how she had lost her friend in an accident and how it could have been prevented, if only someone had intervened. This was his epiphany. He realized that everyone has a personal story about health and safety that they can share. Stories are easy to tell because they come from the heart and stories always resonate with others and make them listen.

James now knew what he needed the management team members to say. From then on, every sponsor of his H&S leadership program began a session by telling *their* H&S story. These stories built leadership credibility and often secured employee buy-in to the message too. In fact, employees loved them, and even started telling them to other people, which got more and more people interested in coming up with their own ideas for health and safety and proactively preventing incidents.

The seven things we have listed above to keep in mind when communicating our H&S message will all contribute to the influence we have on health and safety, and the likelihood that our employees will adopt our defined H&S behaviors. They need to be built into every communication about our H&S program, and every message communicated within it. They also need to be factored into not just what we say, but *how* we say it. Transformational communication needs to be woven into every single element of our program.

Everything our H&S leadership program says and does needs to inspire rather than mandate others to get involved.

Recognizing the need for a different type of communication will change behaviors more quickly than we thought possible. In the next chapter, we will consider one specific H&S behavior, speaking out and speaking up, and how we make sure it is a game changer.

 **Checklist 9**

How to communicate for behavioral change

1. Have you been clear about the behavior you want to see?

2. Is your behavior stated in the positive? Does it say what you want, rather than what you don't want?

3. Have you explained the benefits of the behavior, and why it is so important?

4. Is your message emotional as well as logical?

5. Are you visibly modeling the behavior yourself, leading by example?

6. Are you politely challenging others who are not adopting the required behavior?

7. Is there a reciprocal behavior, for example, a thank you?

8. Have you considered old habits and how they work?

9. Have you thought about how you ensure that new habits are adopted?

10. How will you make your message consistent?

11. Is your communication transformational?

12. Are you speaking the language of empowerment and ownership, rather than of duty and obligation?

 ## Action focus 9

For senior managers:
Assess yourself against the new H&S behaviors, identify any gaps, and commit to role modeling them in a visible way.

For health and safety professionals:
When you are out and about, change your focus to talking about what people are doing right for health and safety rather than what they are doing wrong.

For the communications and engagement manager:
What advice can you give the H&S team on engaging employees in health and safety?

For the HR director:
How can health and safety, and the new behaviors, be incorporated into the employee experience process?

Jason Anker MBE, inspirational speaker

It is really hard to get employees, especially those who work in an office, to understand the relevance of health and safety to them, and the potential impact if it all goes wrong. I think the main problem is the conflicting messages they receive from management.

On one hand, managers stand up once a year and tell the employees that their health and safety is a priority, but on the other hand, employees often haven't seen their manager or supervisor for months. Meanwhile, the day-to-day working environment demands that they focus on just getting the job done, as quickly as possible.

If you want to change behavior on the frontline, managers at all levels need to *be* the change they want to see. It is as simple as that. For me, this is leadership: never asking your people to do something you wouldn't be prepared to do yourself.

Managers need to be seen regularly out on the worksites, getting involved and seeking to understand the day-to-day challenges of their workers. They need to be out there talking and role modeling health and safety and reinforcing rather than confusing the messages coming from top management.

There are two important elements to this.

First, when managers invest time walking the floor, getting to know their people, and praising the safe behaviors, as well as gently pointing out the unsafe ones, they put credit in their emotional bank account. This credit builds up over time, and employees begin to trust them and follow their lead.

Second, this gives managers a chance to have more positive than negative conversations, and this inspires and motivates their people to work better, faster and most importantly, more safely. When managers only ever appear when things have gone wrong, and the conversation is a negative one, you can imagine the impact on the workforce morale, and their health and safety.

Spending time chatting to workers may seem like a big effort, but it is just a matter of scheduling it in. Walking the floor, for say 15 minutes every Monday morning, and creating the space for positive conversations about health and safety, pays dividends. It will help to keep workers healthy and safe and improve productivity.

Finally, this is all crucial to worker wellbeing and mental health, which really comes before everything. If employees are stressed and anxious, they won't work safely. In a nutshell, if the management team wants the whole company to be focused on health and safety, then they need to put in the time with their people. It is not rocket science, but there are no shortcuts. Health and safety is about people, and people need to know you care.

CHAPTER 10

Confidence: Create a speak-up culture for health and safety

Giving people the confidence to speak out regarding H&S concerns is arguably *the* most important part of creating an H&S movement. If our employees don't speak out, how will we know when things are going wrong? If employees don't speak out, how will we prevent accidents and illnesses that are just waiting to happen? If we believe that all accidents are preventable, all it takes is for someone to speak out and take action, to prevent them from happening in the first place.

A speak-out or speak-up culture also has the wider benefit of creating a more transparent culture in a business. There is no doubt that health and safety is a good place to begin creating such a culture.

Getting people to speak out and intervene, when necessary, in the interests of health and safety, is game-changing behavior. When we get this right, we have the power to transform our company culture and our H&S performance. This is because the majority, if not all, of the H&S incidents that happen at work could have been prevented by someone who saw what was about to happen.

Employees on the frontline may well be the most exposed to risk, but they are also the ones who can best mitigate that risk. Our employees are the last line of defense, and intervention or speaking out is the way to bring this line of defense to life.

With a potentially game-changing behavior on our hands, we may need to give this area a bit of extra attention. We must make sure that this message reaches the frontline, so that the associated behavior will start to gain traction. Let's go back a few steps and recap.

To make our H&S leadership program a success, we will have decided on a set of behaviors that we know will work. We are confident about this because they are based on a direct analysis of our own H&S incidents.

Thinking again about John Kotter's book, *Our Iceberg Is Melting* (2017), he says that the first step to achieving a goal is to create a sense of urgency. For the penguins, this was showing the colony the evidence that their iceberg was melting. For us, making sure the behaviors we choose are based on a thorough analysis of our incidents is a good way to get employees to focus on why our H&S behaviors are of urgent importance.

After all, wouldn't you want to adopt a behavior if you knew not doing so might get someone hurt or even killed?

Wouldn't you sit up and take notice if you knew that not behaving in a certain way had caused someone in your company to get hurt?

All our behaviors should be important, or we wouldn't have chosen them. As we said earlier though, one particular behavior has the potential to be a game changer. It has the power to prevent an incident happening, even without all the other behaviors in place. For health and safety, that behavior is *intervention*. By this we mean stopping someone, or stopping a job, to have a conversation, because we perceive that there is a risk, and we need to make sure that no one gets hurt.

Intervention is of extreme importance to health and safety, and to creating a culture that keeps employees healthy and safe. Whatever set of behaviors we have decided on, based on the evidence from our H&S incidents, intervention is sure to be on our list. Why? Because for every H&S incident that ever happened, there was nearly always someone who could have prevented it. All they had to do was intervene. All they had to do was speak up.

Intervening means stopping the people who are about to put themselves at risk. It means speaking up when we are asked to do something that makes us feel uncomfortable in H&S terms, because we are worried about our health, safety or wellbeing, or someone else's. It means stopping work if we can see an accident or health exposure waiting to happen.

Put like that, it sounds simple, but intervention can be tricky for many people.

Intervention may mean pressing pause on work, to tackle an unaddressed H&S issue. Stopping work, however, can be costly. Speaking up may cause offence, or worse lose us our job. This may be our fear, even if it is not a reality, when deciding to speak up. This fear feels very real, as Laura Delizonna points out in an article about psychological safety in 2017:[19]

The brain processes a provocation by a boss, competitive co-worker, or dismissive subordinate as a life-or-death threat. The amygdala, the alarm bell in the brain, ignites the fight-or-flight response, hijacking higher brain centers. This 'act first, think later' brain structure shuts down perspective and analytical reasoning. Quite literally, just when we need it most, we lose our minds.

No one wants to inadvertently provoke someone at work, or to be on the other end of this kind of a reaction if they do.

Intervention takes confidence and courage because we don't always know how it will be received. Speaking up for health and safety is a high-risk activity — almost as high risk as the issue the employee is speaking up about. The risk is psychological rather than physical, but that makes it no less important.

In *Good to Great: Why Some Companies Make the Leap … and Others Don't* (2001),[20] Jim Collins talks of 'red flag mechanisms.' This is where employees can raise a metaphorical red flag when they are not sure of something, or if they want to alert their co-workers to potential issues. By creating the red flag mechanism, a company makes it acceptable to question and challenge the status quo. We need to do the same with health and safety, by making it acceptable for employees to raise a concern.

Heads above the parapet please

Jim was part of the management team of a UK company when it merged with a US competitor. To ensure the merger's success, an integration team was set up, and they got to work identifying the different workstreams required to integrate the key processes across both companies. This work was complex and time consuming, requiring a lot of liaison between different groups of people, across different time zones. The UK team started working later hours to accommodate their US colleagues, and the US people started working earlier hours to accommodate their UK colleagues. This was considerate on both sides, and was done with the best of intentions, but it wasn't good for team wellbeing, as everyone soon became exhausted due to their longer working days.

This issue was recognized and flagged up by a member of the team, who bravely decided to raise the issue with management. Luckily, the management team recognized the significance of this intervention for wellbeing and thanked the team member publicly. This sent a clear message to the rest of the company that results would not be demanded at the expense of employee wellbeing. The integration team might have burned out completely before the end of the integration project if the team member hadn't spoken up when he did.

Fortunately, the right company culture was in place to recognize that wellbeing came first. Everyone in the team felt valued and was now more motivated than ever to find other ways to ensure the successful merger of the two companies. Three years later, the integration of the two companies was judged to have been successful and underpinned by a strong culture that revolved around people welfare.

Despite the perceived barriers in the minds of employees, intervention *has* to happen, because as we said earlier, it is also the last line of defense.

This is precisely why intervention is a game-changing behavior. The simple act of intervention can save a life. So, anything that we can do to support it and make it easier is effort well spent. This is why intervention is the *one* behavior worthy of some extra special attention.

So, we must consider one more crucial factor.

Intervention will become the norm only when we introduce a reciprocal behavior to support it.

That reciprocal behavior means people not only intervening, but those on the receiving end of the intervention thanking them for doing it.

When intervention is welcomed, praised and celebrated, employees are more likely to do it, and *more* employees are likely to do it. This means more incidents can be prevented, and we can create more opportunities to keep our people healthy and safe. Did you intervene during the Covid-19 pandemic when someone wasn't two meters away from you in a queue for takeaway coffee? Did you say something in a supermarket when someone wasn't wearing a face covering? If you were brave enough to speak up, how did the other person react?

When intervention to protect ourselves or someone else isn't welcomed, then it won't happen, which will mean that, sadly, accidents and illnesses still will.

Can you imagine if you plucked up the courage to speak up and intervene regarding health and safety and then got a negative response? How likely would you be to do it again? Not very, I would imagine.

What we are trying to achieve is an environment of psychological safety. This has benefits for the speak-up culture that we want to create, and to the company as a whole. According to research by McKinsey(2021):[21]

The companies that develop the leadership skills and positive work environment that help create psychological safety can reap many benefits, from improved innovation, experimentation and agility to better overall organizational health and performance.

Google also carried out some research on high-performing teams. It discovered that the top driver of high performance was psychological safety.

When we focus on game-changing behavior, we need to make sure that we have closed the loop, so that speaking up is always well received.

If we want to make speaking up central to our H&S culture, we need to put equal emphasis on the reciprocal behavior: thanking, welcoming and praising intervention. All of this will ensure that intervention gets the support it needs to thrive. We need to make sure that our employees feel comfortable speaking up, without fear of adverse reactions, reprisals or blame.

Choosing one game-changing behavior does not mean that we have forgotten the other behaviors; they are all important. What it does mean is that the game-changing behavior must be so well supported that it can become the springboard for all the others.

Speaking up for health and safety is likely to be the most difficult behavior for our employees to adopt, because it requires employees to face potential conflict, head on. At the same time, it is the one behavior that will have the biggest and fastest impact on our H&S culture, and thereby company culture as a whole.

Making it easy for employees to speak up about health and safety needs to be central to our H&S movement.

We have made sure that speaking up for health and safety, our game-changing behavior, is fully supported. Let's move to Part 3 – BAKE, where we make sure our H&S movement gets hundreds, or even thousands, of followers.

⏻ Checklist 10

How to make it easy for employees to speak up and intervene for health and safety

1. Make intervention the key behavior in all your program materials.

2. Make it clear that intervention is the right thing to do.

3. Include a reciprocal behavior for intervention and give it equal prominence to intervention itself.

4. Make intervention the focus of your training for frontline workers, who are the most likely to need to intervene but may find it the most difficult.

5. Understand and make a list of the barriers to intervention that exist: perceptual, company and cultural.

6. Record a video message from a senior stakeholder, authorizing all employees to intervene whenever they perceive a risk.

7. Create a chain of support for speaking up and intervention throughout your company.

8. Make sure that all interventions are backed up by a chain of management.

9. Celebrate all interventions publicly; consider announcing an intervention or speak-up of the month.

10. Consider including the number of interventions as a performance indicator for your program, showing that the behavior is being adopted.

 ## Action focus 10

For senior managers:
How will you let your people know that you want them to speak up for health and safety concerns, and that they will have your support when they do?

For health and safety professionals:
What simple conversational technique could you show employees to help them speak up for health and safety concerns?

For the communications and engagement manager:
How could the company celebrate and recognize interventions for health and safety?

For the HR director:
How could you build a speak-up culture for health and safety into your existing company culture?

Louise Ward, health and safety director

I recently had a bit of a revelation, which was surprising after having worked in health and safety for over 20 years. Over these two decades, I have been involved in numerous safety conversations, initiatives and training programs, but it has only just dawned on me that conversations should have two sides.

All the safety conversation programs that I had been involved with in the past dealt purely with the 'transmit' phase of a conversation: the stepping in or delivery of a message.

But what I recently realized is *that* is not a conversation, it is simply making a statement or giving an instruction. To become a conversation, it requires a second 'receive' phase, where another person hears what has been said, processes it, and then responds or takes action.

So, to be properly effective in developing safe and healthy behavior in the workplace, surely our safety conversation programs should be targeting both the 'transmit' *and* 'receive' phases of a conversation? There is little point preparing people to step in or speak up if we haven't also prepared them to listen actively, discuss curiously and develop a shared understanding, action or conclusion.

'Talk to Me' is the name of the new culture program at my company. It focuses not just on having the courage to step in when something doesn't look right, but also on the character required to accept being challenged and being able to engage in a positive conversation to promote health, safety and wellbeing.

The feedback from this program has been positive so far. It is helping us to drive a step change in culture through engagement and interactive conversation.

Diagram 3 – Putting the 'buzz' in transformational health and safety.

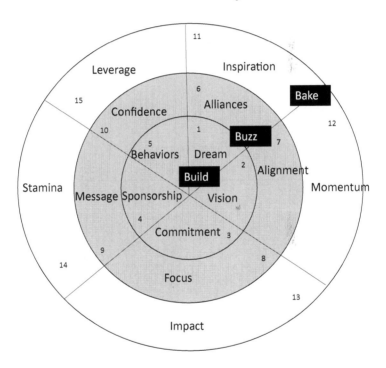

PART 3

BAKE

CHAPTER 11

Inspiration: Get others to join your movement

We have dared to believe that putting health and safety at the heart of our company is the right thing to do. We have cared enough to put all the necessary elements into place. We may have already seen some quick wins. Now it is time to make our progress stick, to bake it into our organization, and to move things up a gear. It is time to use our new focus on H&S leadership to transform our company. We have started our H&S movement, now it is time to inspire others to come on board with us.

To create any kind of behavioral change in companies, whatever their size, a lot of sustained hard work is required. Even with the strongest passion for our cause, and the most worthwhile motivation, we will only get so far by ourselves.

In Chapter 2, we looked at John Kotter's eight-step change model. Step 2 advises "forming a powerful coalition," and we probably already have this in place. The pre-engagement work outlined in Chapter 6 will also have stood us in good stead and given us a valuable network of key stakeholders.

Now it is time to make that network bigger and spread the ownership of health and safety as far and wide as we can.

It is time to get ourselves some reinforcements: we need supporters, champions, cheerleaders, followers and more.

It doesn't matter what we decide to call them; the crucial point is that we need people who are going to adopt our cause as if it were their own. People who will evangelize about it as if their life depended on it, because this is often literally the case. If they do this right, they may well save lives. When we have enough of these reinforcements to rely on, we will have a whole army of change leaders.

Finding them won't be without its challenges, however. Creating change for something popular is easy; just think of the huge queues for the latest Apple iPhone. Health and safety, however, doesn't always get the best press, internally or externally. You will no doubt have read dramatic Christmas headlines about "Elf and safety gone mad!" and that isn't the worst of them, unfortunately.

If we want followers, then we are going to have to up our game. We are going to have to blow not just a breath of fresh air, but in some cases a whole tornado, into the H&S approach we take.

It doesn't matter how much *we* believe in the power of health and safety to transform a company; our people have to believe it too.

Health and safety professionals do not always get the admiration they deserve, but it is important to remember that they are in the business of saving lives. The sad thing is that this work is often appreciated only when our health and safety is under threat. At no time in the last few years has this been so obvious as it was during the Covid-19 pandemic.

We must do everything we can to get ahead of the next threat before it arrives. We need to get ourselves an army of H&S evangelists right now. After all, it is only when disaster strikes that people realize just how much they have taken their H&S function for granted.

One wise, elderly gentleman sitting next to me on a flight a few years ago summed it up quite well by saying, "As long as we have our health, we are millionaires."

So, let us now consider how to build our army. Clearly any new army will need to be trained. To help us with this we can turn to the Deming Model of Quality Management popularized towards the end of the last century by W. Edwards Deming,[22] who was considered to be the father of quality control.

His model advocates that we do the following four things, in this order:

Plan, Do, Check and Act.

First, we need a **Plan**, and planning is often just asking and answering a whole series of questions.

As Deming himself said on the topic of questions, "If you don't know how to ask the right questions, you discover nothing."

Here are some good planning questions, so we can follow Deming's advice and try to "discover everything." At the very least we will discover what we need to do next.

1. What does an H&S champion look like?

2. What do we want them to know?

3. What do we want them to do?

4. How do we want them to feel?

5. What impact will they have on others?

6. What will they need to believe to make all of this happen?

7. What barriers will we need to remove?

8. How many of them will we need to reach the population we need to influence within the required timeframe?

9. Who will train the champions and start the movement? Will it be us, someone else or a small team of people?

As a quick aside, if some of these questions seem a bit strange, don't worry. It may be because some are aimed more at our inner 'doer' and others at our inner 'planner.' Some questions will also reflect the emphasis that we placed on values and beliefs in Chapter 7.

Putting the 'super' into 'super trainer'!

A large UK-based company had acquired a Spanish subsidiary. Corporative initiatives were always slow to reach this part of the business, and the management team of the Spanish business often felt neglected. They were expected to liaise with the head office in English, but at the same time engage their own employees and meet their regulatory commitments in Spanish. Somehow this always ended up doubling their work, and corporative initiatives didn't always get the attention they deserved. When it came to putting health and safety at the heart of the company, however, a special effort was made on both sides, and a formula was found that really worked.

The program manager from head office visited Spain twice, once to train the management team and get them on board, and then a second time to train a small group of employees as 'super trainers.' They were trained in the 'how' as well as the 'what,' translating all the materials and processes into Spanish. They then began their own roll-out to all their centers in Spain. The secret to this success came from Daniel Pink's Motivation 3.0 Model. The Spanish employees knew that they were part of a global purpose; they were given autonomy to do it as they saw fit, and they were also able to master the subject matter, through their super trainer training. This success paved the way for better integration in other areas of the business too.

Six months later, a group of Spanish employees were invited to be involved in a new corporate H&S improvement project, and an idea they came up with turned out to be critical to the results.

The second part of Deming's model concerns the **Do**. We need to make all of this happen, so our to-do list might look something like this:

1. Identify and contact our champions.

2. Give them an experience of the training they will give to others. More than just getting the knowledge, they also need to *feel* a certain way to get motivated and have the right beliefs to ensure the right action.

3. Train them how to deliver the training to others, focusing on Daniel Pink's three pillars of intrinsic motivation: autonomy, mastery, and purpose. Allow them independence, but support them to excel in their new skills, and connect them to the bigger picture.

4. Assess their delivery, coach them to be the best they can be and reward them with certification.

5. Create a training guideline and toolkit; distribute this to our training specialists.

Once our champions are up and running, and the message is getting out there, we will need to move on to the third part of the model, to **Check** how they are doing.

We need a good way of checking how our champions are doing. For this we can look to the four-level model created by Donald Kirkpatrick in the 1950s and published in his book, *Evaluating Training Programs: The Four Levels* (1975).[23] This model is very effective in verifying the effectiveness of training programs.

As before, asking the right questions is so important. Here are some things to consider:

1. Is the training being delivered to the required standard?

2. What feedback are we getting on it?

3. How are people reacting to it and have they understood it?

4. Is this translating into the behavioral change that we want to see in our workforce?

5. What impact is it having on our business results?

If we have got this far, with a plan that has been thought out, delivered and checked back on, then there is only one thing left to do in Deming's model. That is to **Act** on the feedback we are getting.

The challenge is that we need to *keep acting* on the feedback; it is not just a one-off process.

Furthermore, if the feedback isn't forthcoming, then we need to go looking for it. We and our champions can do this by asking some simple but effective questions:

1. What is working?

2. What isn't working?

3. What do we need to change?

We have created an army of followers for our H&S mission. Turn to the next chapter to see how we get them marching forward in unison. It is time to get our H&S movement underway.

⏻ Checklist 11

How to get yourself an army of champions

1. Have you defined the type of person who would make a good H&S champion?

2. Have you made a list of what you want them to know?

3. Have you listed the activities you want them to undertake?

4. What feeling do you want them to have as a result?

5. What impact do you expect they will have on others?

6. What beliefs will they need to hold to make this happen?

7. What barriers will you need to remove?

8. How many of them will you need to reach your target population?

9. Who will train them and when?

 **Action focus 11**

For senior managers:

How can you free up would-be champions for the new H&S focus so that the right people can dedicate a percentage of their time to it, alongside their operational roles?

For health and safety professionals:

How can you get people from outside health and safety interested in championing your cause? What plan do you need in place to attract the best?

For the communications and engagement manager:

How can you help the H&S team promote their champion campaign internally?

For the HR director:

What opportunities are there to include expertise in H&S leadership in your talent management program?

Karl Simons OBE, health, safety, security and wellbeing director

The first step in getting the whole company focused on health and safety is to decide to create a culture of care and make this an essential part of business strategy and decision-making. Companies, once they grow, start to have complex systems and processes for health and safety. Sometimes they need to have this complexity to keep people safe. To take it to the next level, however, means going back to basics, and that simply means caring about one another.

A culture of care is also a culture of inclusion, and to create and sustain a culture that has both elements requires many different considerations. There are, however, two key ingredients that allow the company to move towards a culture where people feel great about their workplaces. They are stable leadership and constant waves of initiatives.

Inspiring people to feel great about their workplace is key to health and safety, and to everything else, and it all starts with trust in leadership. Trust takes time to build, however, and companies that continuously change leaders and structures can see their hard-won 'trust bank account' rapidly empty across their workforce.

For trust and integrity to last, leaders need not only to 'live' the daily successes and failures of health and safety, to inspire the right behaviors in their employees, but also be prepared to do this, not only day in, day out, but year, in year out.

To inspire others to get involved in health and safety takes constancy and consistency, and that is why waves of initiatives, year after year, really work. Leadership teams need to be guided by employee feedback in doing so and be prepared to take risks. Not every initiative will stick, but many will, as employees become H&S champions and embed them in their workplaces.

In my current company, we have introduced around 20 H&S initiatives every year for the past eight years, and this, alongside sustained leadership support, has been instrumental in convincing employees that health and safety is so important that they go on to individually champion the cause. All this adds up to a strong H&S culture, which has led to improvements in our H&S performance indicators across the board.

CHAPTER 12

Momentum: Make your H&S movement a reality

We are now fully into the Bake phase of creating a movement for health and safety, and we have reached the part where the rubber really hits the road, testing out our carefully laid plans in the real world.

It is time to give our employees the training they need, to begin to make the difference we want them to make. We need to give them the training to feel inspired and equipped to be leaders for health and safety. It is time to fasten our seatbelts and get ready to go full throttle – safely, of course.

Some employees will be easier to convince than others, but if we want them to change their behavior, which we do, then we are going to have to create some epiphanies and eureka moments.

"I'm sorry," I can hear you saying, "what does that mean?"

Epiphany – you know, when you have a moment of sudden and great revelation or realization.

Eureka moments – when you suddenly understand a previously incomprehensible problem or concept.

Stay with me; all will become clear shortly.

Let's think about the people who are going to attend our training. They are going to do something differently at the end of it only if they realize for themselves during the training that something has to change.

Do you remember in Chapter 10, when we looked again at John Kotter's eight-step change model, and considered how Step 1 was about creating a sense of urgency? Well, this sense of urgency is something we are going to have to create for our H&S program. It is about creating the rationale for change, as we discussed earlier, and also about creating urgency within the individual.

Psychologist Nathaniel Branden apparently once said, "The first step toward change is awareness. The second is acceptance."

It is up to us and our army of followers to raise awareness of the need for change in our employees, and to move them to acceptance of this need.

Once we have achieved these two things, for every employee that sits our H&S leadership training, it will become far easier to lead them to action.

There's an epiphany up your sleeve

The H&S leadership workshop for the management team was nearing its end point. Having spoken for four hours about her best behavioral change techniques, Monique realized that she still had a few perplexed faces in the room. A couple of people had been expecting something different, and they still didn't quite 'get it.' They still hadn't reached the point where they realized that they *had* to do something differently, right now, because their employees' lives depended on it.

Sensing the problem, she decided to go off-script for a moment. She moved to the flipchart, which was in the direct field of vision of the skeptical few. She drew three numbers on the flipchart and used them to illustrate her own personal safety story. After just a minute, her audience, including the skeptics, were empathizing with her emotions, understanding the importance of the story. As she finished speaking, she ripped off the flipchart paper to emphasize the life that had tragically been lost.

Then Monique grabbed a fresh sheet of paper, to represent the chance to do things differently in future. She saw their eyes mist over; they were visibly moved. Finally, she had provided the epiphany they needed. She had no doubt that the penny had dropped, and they now understood the importance of the H&S message. At the end of the workshop, one of the managers came up to speak to Monique privately. "Now I get it," he said, "and I'm so sorry about your friend."

This is exactly what a great coach would do. First, they would ask some relevant questions to increase awareness and acceptance of the need for change. Their final question would ensure that their team had the necessary commitment to act on it.

So, if we want our training to deliver the behavioral change that we need, we have to become good trainers and facilitators, and great coaches too. We must arm ourselves with a coach's toolkit: some excellent questions.

Let's go back now to those epiphanies and eureka moments and find out how you can recognize them.

People don't usually stand up in the middle of a training session with their arms above their head and their fists clenched, shouting, "That's it! That's what I need to do!"

Perhaps they will now? Arguably the epiphany for health and safety has already happened, during the Covid-19 pandemic, when we watched the lives that we had taken for granted be completely stripped back because of the risk from a deadly virus.

Anyway, back to our training room, if anyone *has* jumped up and shouted about having an epiphany in the middle of your training session, then please do let me know. This would be a story worth hearing, for sure.

Of course, social norms dictate that anyone doing anything of the sort in the workplace would get an interesting stare at the very least, but does that mean that epiphanies aren't happening? Not at all. Especially not on the training courses we are going to be delivering for H&S leadership. There will be epiphanies all over the place if we have got our tone exactly right.

Epiphanies and eureka moments happen more often than we think, right in front of our eyes. They may not be obvious, but we can still see them, in the micro-movements of a person's facial gestures and body language. All we have to do is look out for them, and then help the person having the epiphany to make the most of it.

As soon as we can feel that our employees' minds are open to change, that is the moment to suggest the way to change. The moment the unconscious mind is open to suggestion is the moment people become open to doing something in a different way.

When our training delivers not only knowledge, but also the inspiration for employees to improve themselves, and to help their companies do the same, then we are on to a winner.

So how do we do this?

You may be thinking "Isn't it hard enough just producing and delivering the content?"

Getting this far will have been hard, but with a little extra thought and effort, we can deliver so much more. Especially armed with a checklist of questions to help us.

Before you read ahead, try to remember these two important facts:

1. Maya Angelou famously said, "People will forget what you did, they will forget what you said, but they will never forget the way you made them feel."

2. This quote from my first book, *Employee Confidence*, is also worth considering: "People will only change when they *want* to make a difference, *believe* they can make a difference, and *know* they can make a difference."

So, it is not *all* about the content, although of course that is still important.

Here is the checklist of what else matters:

1. How many different learning styles do our content and language cater for? By this I mean visual, auditory, kinesthetic and auditory digital. By talking across the whole spectrum of learning styles, we are more likely to engage our whole audience, and engagement is the first step to change.

2. Does our content have emotion interspersed with logic? Give people the evidence to change, by all means, and give them the facts; but remember that people also make decisions and take action based on emotion. How will we get that emotion across?

3. Have we clearly defined not only our content, but also what our audience needs to believe to be able to take action on it? How will our language make this belief clear, and instill this belief in others?

4. How do we want our audience to feel as a result of our training; what feeling will lead them to the behavioral change we want, and what in our training will make them feel that way? How and when will we transmit this feeling to our audience?

5. Is our training linked to our vision and is our vision clearly stated in our training? Are we constantly linking back to it?

6. Stories are a powerful mechanism for change, so do we have any stories in our training that might inspire the change we want? How good are our storytelling skills?

7. Does our training give people the capability to change? Will it give them the knowledge and the confidence that they personally can make a difference, in their own special way? How will we instill this confidence in our trainees?

8. Are we following up on the training, to give our participants the support they need to keep the behavioral change going, because changing behaviors and habits takes hard work and persistence? Who will be there for them when they falter? Are we making this clear in our delivery?

9. Have we built timeouts into our training? When the brain is overloaded, a change of environment can often allow the eureka moment or epiphany to happen.

The above list isn't exhaustive, but incorporating these nine points could transform our training into an experience our employees won't forget.

If it is behavioral change that we want, it all starts with that epiphany or eureka moment.

And if it is behavioral change for health and safety, where the desired behaviors keep people safe and healthy, the stakes have never been higher.

Our training needs to bring epiphanies and eureka moments to our participants, as well as being the best training they have ever attended.

Why not set the bar high and make this your goal now?

We now know the secrets to training that inspires people to change their behavior for health and safety. Next let's measure the impact of our program. Has it become a movement yet?

⏻ Checklist 12

The key components of training for behavioral change

1. Materials to engage all learning styles.

2. A message that contains emotion as well as logic.

3. An inherent belief that the facilitator will pass on to their audience.

4. A defined feeling that it needs to invoke in its audience.

5. Reference to an ambitious vision.

6. Lots of stories.

7. Confidence-building opportunities.

8. Follow-up and support after the training.

9. Timeouts during the training.

Action focus 12

For senior managers:
Commit your time to attending one of the new H&S leadership workshops, so that you experience it fully.

For health and safety professionals:
Set up a listening session with a sample of your employees, and brainstorm with them all the reasons why they aren't engaged in health and safety right now.

For the communications and engagement manager:
What support can you give to the H&S team in producing content for their workshops that helps engage all learning styles?

For the HR director:
What resources can the H&S team leverage from your training function to help them organize and deliver their workshops, and train others to do the same?

Mônica Ximenes de Lima Mesquita, health, safety and environment director

I have led the health and safety function in several companies. For me, there are three main challenges to overcome when trying to get the entire company focused on health and safety, while keeping the risks to a minimum. The goal is behavioral change, but it is a common misconception that this is only about the worker. To turn health and safety into a movement in a company, you need to consider individual *and* company behavior.

The first step is to get every single employee not just to know but to *truly understand* that they are responsible for health and safety in their workplaces, and what they need to do with that responsibility. This means finding a way to make employees realize that health and safety is relevant to them and making clear what behaviors are expected of them. It means influencing employees to swap their unsafe behaviors for safe ones.

Having secured their commitment, the second step is to get them to realize that health and safety is not just about having the right tools to control the hazards and risks, but also about 'owning' the processes. I have been involved in behavioral-based safety programs, which provide a mechanism for employees to take ownership of, and drive improvement in, the health and safety of their workplaces. It allows them to work together to eliminate hazards.

At a company level, it means understanding that human beings are prone to error, and that there are things we can do at the managerial level to reduce the likelihood of errors occurring. With this understanding comes an acceptance that when our employees err, or take unnecessary risks, it is often because we as a company have set them up to do so.

The only way to address this is by taking a full-company approach to H&S behaviors and enabling this at all levels, so that the whole system is set up and designed for safe behaviors, not just the frontline workplaces. This is the third step.

What we are talking about here is alignment on the culture we want to see for health and safety in our companies. When a strong H&S culture from top to bottom underpins the employee-driven behavioral change initiative, the whole company is focused on health and safety, and the impact on performance can be remarkable.

CHAPTER 13

Impact: Measure the difference you make

We have built and buzzed. We have started to train. We are hoping to bake our messages so deeply into our company that they make transformational changes. We are even hoping that our H&S mission might become so powerful that it becomes a company movement. Maybe the best movement our company has ever seen.

But how will we know if we have done this?

How will we prove our transformation to those who need to know? To those who want to believe in us, and to those who secretly hoped that we would fail? Yes, sadly we will always have our naysayers, our "NoNo's" of the penguin colony.

How will we show other managers the difference that we have made to our company?

How will we prove that the business case we sold to them at the very beginning has become a reality in our company?

Even if we have only just started training employees in H&S leadership, we will be ready to see our new cohorts beginning to make a difference as H&S leaders. We know that while we may see some quick wins, reaching the whole company and seeing a significant impact, especially if the company is large, is going to take time.

Time is something that you and the other managers in your company don't always have. Even if you do, you may prefer to give it to other priorities.

Only a few weeks after the roll-out of our long-term H&S leadership program begins, our management team will want to see some evidence of success. So, we need to plan for this, long before our first training session has been delivered.

As a manager or change leader embarking upon a program like this, we can often get so caught up in planning and implementing that we forget to plan for success. It is so important to do this right from the start, *before* the program implementation begins, because we need something against which to measure our success.

What we need is a benchmark to measure where we are right now, before our employees are exposed to our program and start to change. That way we can measure the full extent of the difference we made (and of course get the credit for it).

With this in mind, I do hope you got as far as this chapter before you went too far in your implementation.

So, what is our starting point? What is the status quo and how do we measure it?

The first thing to note is that a program focused on H&S leadership is a cultural change program. The aim is to raise awareness of the importance of health and safety among all employees, encouraging them to adopt safe working practices and challenging those that aren't. This is H&S leadership.

The second thing to know is that employee perceptions drive behavior.

And these are the perceptions that matter in the mind of the employee:

1. How important is health and safety in my company?

2. How committed is the management team to this?

3. Is my health and safety the priority of my line manager, above all else?

4. Would my line manager and their manager support me if I raised a health and safety issue?

Think about yourself as an employee now. To how many of these questions would you respond positively?

When employee perceptions regarding the above questions are in the affirmative, employees won't hesitate to behave safely and to challenge others who don't.

They will behave as H&S leaders because they know this is what is expected of them. They know that health and safety is a strategic priority, management is committed to it, and this has filtered down to their line manager. Their line manager in turn makes it clear that health and safety is the top priority – despite the pressures of cost and schedule – and that their team is empowered to speak up if they perceive that there is an H&S risk.

Perceptions, then, are the starting point for cultural change.

When perceptions are as described above, and joined up across the company, the cultural shift can be extremely powerful. This isn't always the case, however.

These perceptions are what we want to measure, starting with where the company is at right now.

Before we start our H&S leadership program in earnest, we first need to benchmark perceptions in the company. To do this, we need to commission a survey, asking everyone in the company to answer a series of questions, which will gauge their perceptions.

The four questions set out above are a good starting point, but we will probably need specialist advice to get our questions absolutely right, as the language used is really important.

There also needs to be a question to assess the perceptions of employees about the importance their line manager places on health and safety. We want employees to feel that their direct hierarchy values health and safety above all else. If they don't, this will be our starting point for cultural change.

When we conduct this survey of the existing H&S culture in our company, you can expect the percentage of managers perceived to place a high level of importance on health and safety to be low. If it weren't, why would we have decided to introduce an H&S leadership program? Clearly there are improvements to be made, which is no doubt reflected in a consistent number of H&S incidents in our company, with human behavior as the root cause.

Take note also that a declining trend in incidents will be the first thing you and other managers will ask to see, as proof that our H&S leadership program is working. This isn't, however, what our program will directly impact, so we need to make this clear from the start.

All things being equal, H&S leadership has the potential to directly impact H&S performance, but in most companies, all things are *not* equal. There are so many variables impacting H&S performance that it is impossible to isolate the impact of one, unless we focus on one closed environment.

It is better, therefore, to focus on what our program *can* directly impact: perceptions about health and safety and the company's attitude to it. This can be measured annually to demonstrate the cultural shift.

It is only as our cultural shift happens that we would expect to see a declining trend in H&S incidents over time. We also need to caveat this result with the fact that declining incidents will be the result of many health and safety related factors, not just our H&S leadership program.

Of course, we may want to attribute a declining trend in incidents to our H&S leadership program in the short term, but what happens if the incidents start to go up again? This is entirely possible, due to other factors impacting on this trend.

Do we want other managers to think that the H&S leadership program isn't working, and withdraw support for it, throwing all our good work out of the window?

This is why cultural shift, assessed through surveying employee perceptions, is the best and most reliable measure of success for our H&S leadership program.

We need to consider our key performance indicators (KPIs), the measurable values that demonstrate how effectively a company is achieving its key business objectives.

We mentioned earlier that it may be possible to see quick wins for our program, and these will be important, to calm our nerves, while we maintain the belief and constancy required.

With this in mind, here are some other ways to measure the impact of our H&S leadership program:

1. **Training numbers.** The first stage of any cultural change is awareness, so this can be a good measure of success in the early stage of the program. Knowing that employees have been trained in the new H&S leadership program will give us an important early indicator of success. We can also set ourselves an early objective of say 90% of our employees being trained by a certain future date. While not explicitly reliable, having a report of training numbers also allows us to correlate these figures with other data, showing potential links. For example, if our incident trend is downwards, while our training numbers are moving upwards, this could be a good sign.

2. **Adoption of behaviors.** If we identify and communicate a clear set of behaviors required from all employees, that is, a clear definition of what an H&S leader does, then the adoption of these behaviors becomes visible. Without evidence of return on investment, managers are comforted when out on their leadership tours because they can see the behaviors in action.

3. **Training feedback.** We need to design our feedback forms in a way that indicates how employees feel at the end of our training, and how likely they are to change behavior

and take action as a result. This will give us a short-term indicator to report to management regularly, alongside our numbers of employees trained. For example, we could say something like, "Out of 1,000 employees trained, 80% said they would behave more safely as a result, and 70% said they would now feel confident to challenge someone who wasn't behaving safely." A good feedback form, with results compiled regularly, can provide useful feedback about employee perceptions as soon as they have finished their training.

The final point to remember when reporting the impact of our program is that it is the leading indicators, which predict future conditions, that are important here. The lagging indicators assess the current state of the business.

Leading indicators are measures of proactive and preventive activities designed to keep our people safe. For us, these include things like numbers of people trained or the number of interventions recorded for safety. When these numbers start to grow, we can feel confident that keeping people safe is not only possible, but also highly probable. Make sure that your management team knows and understands the importance of measuring past health and safety incidents, as well as the proactive, preventive action being taken to avoid them now.

Our H&S leadership program will encompass a whole spectrum of positive activity, which is all designed to be preventive, rather than reactive, towards health and safety. It is intended to manage the risks that our company's activities bring about. It can be summed up quite simply as 'doing the right thing.'

Thank heavens for Kirkpatrick

Gosia worked in learning and development and had been designing and delivering leadership programs for years. The program manager for the new H&S leadership program, Luis, approached her and asked for her help. How could he best measure the impact of the training he was about to roll out company-wide? Gosia recommended redesigning the participant feedback form to align it with the Kirkpatrick model, which they used regularly in their department.

By working together, Gosia and Luis were able to measure the following four things for each participant, after each workshop:

1. Did they enjoy the training?

2. Did they learn a lot from it?

3. Did they understand the new H&S leadership behaviors?

4. Would they apply them, because if so, this would undoubtedly increase H&S and maybe even other areas of business performance?

Using the Kirkpatrick model was a game changer in the success of Luis's H&S leadership program. When the management team asked whether the program was starting to change behavior, Luis could show that 90% of workshop participants said they would apply the new H&S leadership behaviors. That was some outcome.

So, if your management team mentions a lack of movement in your incident trends, you can say this:

> The question is, are we doing the right things for health and safety? The things that give us more confidence that we can keep people safe, in spite of the daily challenges. Hand on heart, I believe that we are. The activities we are undertaking all stem from a deeply rooted belief that we can and will prevent all incidents. To paraphrase Henry Ford, "Whether we think we can or think we can't, we are absolutely right." A declining incident trend may give us comfort in the short term, but knowing that we are doing all that we can to prevent incidents is what will allow us to sleep well at night.

Hopefully, a powerful statement such as this will stop any criticism in its tracks, as all managers will agree that doing the right thing is the *only* thing to do.

We have discovered how to prove that our H&S leadership program is making a difference. Now for the difficult part: making it stick.

 **Checklist 13**

Finding the right KPIs for your program

1. Do you have a KPI that is quantitative?

2. Do you have a KPI that is qualitative?

3. Do you have a balance between leading and lagging indicators?

4. Do your KPIs reflect both quick wins and long-term successes?

5. Will your KPIs encourage employees to focus on the right things?

6. Are your KPIs easy for managers to understand?

7. Are your KPIs easy to measure?

8. Will your employees get behind them?

9. Do your KPIs measure behavioral and cultural change?

 Action focus 13

For senior managers:
Brief your H&S team about what you need from a KPI; what makes a good KPI for you?

For health and safety professionals:
Get a meeting with your senior management team to ask them what their expectations are for the return on their investment in H&S leadership.

For the communications and engagement manager:
Which company communication channels can be used to make progress against H&S KPIs more visible to employees?

For the HR director:
Which measures of success in company training can be used to guide the H&S team's use of H&S training program KPIs?

Pierre-Arnaud Delattre, senior safety specialist

In my experience, the challenge in measuring success in relation to health and safety lies in finding the right things to measure across the right timescales. This is even more challenging for the leadership part of health and safety. How do we measure the quality of someone's leadership? Businesses run on KPIs, and we need to choose the ones that bring health and safety, and business priorities, together at the same time.

We also need to consider both lagging and leading indicators, where we look back at the safety incidents that have already happened and forward to the proactive things we are doing to improve safety culture. Since H&S culture is never a quick fix, the leading indicators need to be trended over longer periods than most companies are usually comfortable with.

When implementing H&S leadership programs in the real world, two key ingredients are essential for success. First, consultation with key stakeholders to establish the right KPIs. Second, the flexibility to be able to work with different data types. This is because lagging indicators will be found in quantitative data and leading indicators in qualitative data, because doing the right things for safety, like leadership and communication, are not easy to measure in plain numbers.

The main point of all this data is to prove that your efforts are making a difference. With more intangible things, like H&S leadership and communication, it isn't always easy to measure return on investment. But measure it we must. That's why I turned to the learning and development industry for inspiration, where the experts have been measuring these kind of intangibles for years. I discovered that they weren't measuring return on investment (ROI) but return on expectations (ROE).

This discovery led me to engage directly with program sponsors to map out their expectations for an ROI in any kind of long-term H&S leadership activity requiring a significant outlay of resources. This often required a leap of faith on the part of the sponsor, but being clear on expectations upfront made it easier. It meant that I was able to influence those expectations to ensure they were appropriate, long-term and realistic. I could give a steer, for example, on what their investment might tangibly make a difference to, for example avoiding the terrible cost of a fatality.

The leap of faith I mention above comes only when the sponsor holds health and safety as a personal value, when they are educated on what is possible, and when they know that health and safety is good for business. This is where we often have a slight chicken and egg situation, because the sponsor may not be in this position until they have experienced the training for themselves.

My final word of advice then is to train your key managers first. Having opened their minds to the impact that a program like this could have in their area of the business, sit down with them and discuss their expectations, so you can make sure that your program delivers on them.

CHAPTER 14

Stamina: Make sure the difference sticks

Putting health and safety at the heart of our company is a long-term investment, but this often runs counter to company expectations. Managers like you, faced with constant change and short-term challenges, find themselves needing to make decisions quickly and are eager to see a return on their investment.

Health and safety, however, is not a short-term investment, particularly in a large company. While it may be possible to see quick wins on one site, or in one department or team, company-wide results will take time to become visible. This is because results happen only when everyone is aligned. The more global your company is, the harder it is to get everyone on to the same page.

It is up to us, as the changemaker for H&S in our company, to understand this. We need to manage the expectations of all our managers, as we said in the previous chapters, and plan for this.

First and foremost, what does a sustainable H&S leadership program look like?

What makes it a movement – a force for good – that is truly unstoppable?

A sustainable H&S program is one where incremental gains are achieved and start to become visible after several years of concerted effort. It may also be that no signs of success are seen *at all* during this time. This is when belief and constancy are really important. Belief that doing the right things will eventually bear fruit, and constancy of message and action, even in the face of an apparent lack of progress.

It is also one where regular rejuvenation efforts are required, when existing messages run stale or start to fall on deaf ears. This usually happens once all our employees have been trained, and the timeframe for this will depend on the size of our company.

Once the initial novelty has worn off, how do we keep that sense of urgency in people's minds?

We saw this challenge at first hand during the Covid-19 pandemic, when 'lockdown fatigue' set in. The risk from the virus was still there, but all over the world, people struggled to keep their focus on following the rules.

For large companies, it may take years to reach our most remote populations. For small companies, our messages will reach saturation point quickly.

Where companies are fragmented or operate in silos, it may also be the case that some areas get trained quickly but other parts much more slowly. This will inevitably create disparities in awareness levels across the board.

Whatever the makeup or size of our company, we will need to cut our cloth accordingly and plan for the second version of our program. Be ready to relaunch your program and reboot your movement as soon as it is likely that new material will be required.

Nothing in life stands still and our program, like anything else in business, will need to adapt and evolve. Our employees will not be standing still either; some people will have moved on and others will have joined. Those who remain will have an appetite for something new.

First and foremost, then, making our program sustainable means planning for its second evolution. It doesn't need to be radically different; in fact, it should maintain the same vision and the same key messages. It should, however, update employees on success so far and tell them about the next milestones. It should also incorporate latest leadership thinking.

Second, remember that it is neither practical nor sustainable from a resource perspective to keep relaunching our program. This can happen only every two years at most, so we need to find other ways to embed the learning we teach.

Ensuring that the learning in our program is embedded and the behaviors advocated are adopted is the essence of our program. This alone will ensure that its sustainability is self-generating.

For this, you may want to consider the Kirkpatrick model of training effectiveness which we mentioned earlier and build it into your program.

A new buzz in town

The H&S team at an energy company was proud to have an industry-leading H&S leadership program. It was so successful that clients and suppliers wanted to buy it, and the leadership behaviors advocated were even beginning to take root in other parts of the business. The program was five years in, and had more than exceeded expectations, but suddenly things seemed to go a bit stale. Employees were asking for new content and some divisions were reporting training completion figures of more than 90%. At the same time, there was a feeling that people were forgetting what they had learned.

So, the H&S team brought in a coaching expert, and they designed a coaching program to train H&S coaches to follow up on the content learned within the H&S leadership program. The team managed to create a new buzz around health and safety, while at the same time ensuring its longevity. And when the H&S team was looking for evidence of the impact of its work, it was able to cite a long-term improvement in H&S performance, with a significant uptick after the introduction of the coaching program.

With every training session we deliver, we need to know our employees' reactions to it, the learning they take away, the behaviors adopted and the results. By this we mean the results delivered to the business.

Only then can we adjust our program to keep learning and keep it in tune with the needs of our company.

There is a further and final element to consider in the sustainability picture, and that is the rate at which people forget the learning gleaned from a training session, if there isn't a follow-up.

The CIPD (Chartered Institute of Personnel and Development) in the UK reported on the issue of training follow-up in its *People Management* magazine, citing some interesting research by Ask Europe, a behavioral change consultancy. The research findings showed that training needs to be followed up on for at least 13 weeks afterwards to be effective, with the implication that if not, the learning would be lost in this timeframe. But what if they lost it even more quickly than this?

This is where the content in our program will play a role. If our training program is designed and delivered for maximum impact, as discussed in the previous chapters, then the likelihood is far higher that our employees will retain the information and embed the learning without follow-up.

Ensuring that our H&S leadership program is sustainable needs knowledge and planning. Now let's see whether we can get our H&S movement to spill over into other performance areas.

 **Checklist 14**

How to make your H&S leadership program sustainable

1. Define excellence – what does a sustainable program look like?

2. Identify your quick wins.

3. Plan for a second evolution of your program – when will your first round of training be complete?

4. Create a mechanism for your foundational behaviors to be embedded.

5. Identify routes for the foundational behaviors to be deployed.

6. Create a mechanism to follow up on your training, for example, through individual and group coaching.

7. Design refresher courses to complement the main program.

8. Consider 'lunch and learn' training sessions with rotating ownership, so that others take ownership of the program.

9. Make sure that you measure the extent to which your learning is being embedded — try using the Kirkpatrick model.

 Action focus 14

For senior managers:
Ask your H&S team for one-, three- and five-year plans for integrating H&S leadership into your business, with the outcomes at each stage.

For health and safety professionals:
When you design your H&S program, with its associated behaviors, be sure to design a mechanism to enable employees to embed those behaviors.

For the communications and engagement manager:
Offer your creative design expertise to bring the new H&S behaviors to life visually.

For the HR director:
Offer your learning and development expertise to assist the H&S team with the design of its program feedback forms.

Ann McGregor, head of global safety and resilience strategy

The secret to making any focus on health and safety impactful and sustainable is to make sure that the cascade of your dedicated H&S program has no end point. You can plan for this right from the start and do it in several different ways. If you are clever about it, your H&S program will become fully integrated into the training and communications fabric of your business and become self-sustaining. Once the buzz of your program launch has ebbed, and your initial cascade is complete – from CEO or MD to frontline employees – you'll need a variety of methods for keeping your message, behaviors and activities going.

One of the key ways to embed health and safety over the long term is to ensure that your H&S content forms part of the overall employee experience, starting with on-boarding and induction. This is something many companies are starting to do. Be proactive to ensure your program is not a 'fly by night.' What employees experience throughout their time in the company is arguably a key part of the culture you are driving, through a focus on health and safety.

It is also useful to get your program content referenced from other training programs in your company, wherever there is a relevant point to do so. Get in touch with your company training counterparts, study the training catalog with them and reach out to content owners to make this happen. This will ensure that your H&S content is not solely dependent on your delivering it and will create a natural pipeline of interest for it.

Make your program 'sticky' by creating more opportunities for your employees to drive it, so that it takes on a life of its own. Things like creating a 'community of best practice,' which you can support from the center, or an ongoing drip feed of new and refreshed H&S content and information around your program, to keep it current and relevant. Partner with your communications colleagues to make this part of a long-term and strategic engagement strategy. Ask them to infuse your messages into town hall and other meetings, and company-wide campaigns. This is a subtle and powerful way to integrate your program into the business. Creating such communities will allow informal H&S leaders and champions to emerge, driving the program forward with passion and authenticity.

Think about how to keep your learning around health and safety alive. Put in place a mechanism to follow up on all the H&S leadership sessions you run, so you maintain momentum after the initial buzz fades. One way of doing this is to break your program content down into bite-size chunks, which can be shared through online interactive workshop sessions. Include regular case studies and stories that prove the H&S message is alive and show its relevance to the company.

Finally, identify progress activities and milestones as 'leading indicators' which can be built into the employee appraisal process. This will motivate every employee to contribute in their own particular way, as appropriate to their role and position in the company. They will feel part of the H&S vision and culture because they can see how they are directly able to contribute to achieving it.

CHAPTER 15

Leverage: Let your business be transformed

Once we have a successful and sustainable H&S leadership program, other managers and other companies will start to notice. The skills and capabilities we have given employees for health and safety are now not only being used in an H&S context. We are teaching people to be leaders for the topic of health and safety, but their leadership skills are not exclusive to health and safety. Leadership skills are leadership skills, wherever they are developed, and of course they are going to spill over into other areas.

Once we teach people to speak up for health and safety, they are going to do the same for other important issues.

When employees feel confident enough to challenge issues they feel strongly about, they are going to do this for every issue, not just for health and safety.

When employees want to do what is right, they are going to intervene – not just for health and safety, but every time it is the right thing to do.

If people decide to follow the rules for health and safety, they are going to do this for everything, because they now understand the power of collective action.

When employees lead health and safety by asking great open questions, and by listening a lot more, this is an approach they can't help but take back into their day jobs.

The only difference between leadership in health and safety and leadership in other contexts is that for health and safety it has the potential to save lives, and that makes a big difference.

What it means is that leadership in the context of health and safety has a lot at stake, but that doesn't make it easy.

Leading for health and safety means:

1. being prepared to stand by the safe way of working, regardless of competing pressures

2. being prepared to stand by the safe way of working, regardless of the potential repercussions for the person speaking out

3. standing by your values, which isn't always easy to do.

This is why I always say, "If you can lead health and safety, you can lead anything."

Nowhere on the corporate agenda is there an issue as challenging to lead on as health and safety.

This is why leadership skills in the context of health and safety are a route to leadership in other parts of our company. Let's use them to take our company to the next level. The question is, how do we do this?

Let's first take an inventory of the leadership skills possessed by an H&S leader.

An H&S leader should always use transformational leadership as their approach. This is important because research suggests that this approach has a strong impact on H&S culture and, in turn, on H&S performance.

To achieve transformational leadership, managers need to lead in a way that brings out the best in individuals and in groups. They need to lead in a way that allows everyone to fulfill, and even go beyond, their expected potential.

To bring out the best in people, they need to do four things:

1. Have a strong cause or purpose and be prepared to stand by it.

2. Be charismatic and influential in painting a vision of what the cause stands to achieve.

3. Connect with every member of the team individually and tap into their strengths.

4. Challenge each individual to be better, to do better, to think differently and to go the extra mile.

When we build an army of H&S leaders in our company, we are effectively building an army of transformational leaders. And since we said that transformational leaders act more like coaches, we now have an opportunity to build a coaching culture in our company.

This coaching culture – where employees listen to each other and challenge each other's thinking, through open questions – underpins a strong H&S culture. It also becomes a springboard for high performance in other areas.

Our H&S leaders now have leadership skills and coach-like qualities, which enable them to form a culture that can be leveraged across our entire company in support of all business activities and any major new initiative.

How can we strengthen this budding coaching culture so that it starts to have a real impact on employee motivation, engagement and productivity?

How can we make asking good questions a habit and not simply an add-on, if time allows?

This speak-up disease is catching on

The CEO of an insurance company had gone out on something of a limb five years ago, by telling all his employees, clients and shareholders, that their company would be putting health and safety before any other business imperative. There had been a serious accident at the company, which meant that he felt he had no other choice, but it was still a gamble back then, and he knew it.

Fortunately, the gamble had paid off, and the CEO was feeling rather pleased with himself as a result. Not only had the company achieved a long-term reduction in health and safety incidents, but things had improved in some rather unexpected other ways too. As he stood in front of a podium delivering a keynote speech to the biannual industry conference, he had this to say to inspire others in the industry:

> Some years ago, we introduced a behavioral approach for health and safety, asking our people to challenge anyone found not doing the right thing for safety. This approach really worked. Now we have employees who are prepared to speak up and challenge anything that isn't right. This wonderful speak-up disease has spread like wildfire. Now my people have the courage to challenge our suppliers, clients and partners as well – not just about health and safety issues, but on other things such as project scope, cost, wellbeing or simply anything they don't think is right. This has been amazing to see.

Fast forward five years, and employees of the company think nothing of challenging work methods, having been taught a way to do it that never causes offence. A suggestion program for improved work methods has caught on, and has reduced annual operating costs by 15%.

How can we make coaching something that our company *is*, rather than something it simply *does*?

Coaching is all about excellence in communication.

One thing is for sure: every part of a company suffers from flaws in communication, and every part of a company benefits from excellent communication.

We don't need to train everyone as professional coaches; we just need to teach them the ethos of coaching. How to ask good questions which encourage the recipient to think differently and come up with their own positive solutions.

Just having a few good questions that employees can use as H&S leaders can make a world of difference. As demonstrated by Michael Bungay Stanier in his great book, *The Coaching Habit: Say Less; Ask More & Change the Way You Lead Forever* (2016),[24] the simplest of questions can also be the most powerful.

H&S leadership fosters great communication among individuals and lets it grow into a culture that can make a real difference, to every area of the business.

 **Checklist 15**

How to turn H&S leadership into a coaching culture in your company

1. Create a compelling vision – the same one you have established for health and safety.

2. Define the behaviors that will make that vision a reality and around which employees will be coached – the ones you have defined for your H&S vision.

3. Convince all people managers to role model these behaviors.

4. Create a mechanism for people managers to assess themselves against these behaviors – a self-coaching exercise.

5. Deploy trained coaches to coach management on these behaviors.

6. Train all employees in basic coaching techniques and active listening.

7. Give your employees a set of simple but powerful coaching questions for health and safety.

8. Communicate the required behaviors to all employees.

9. Embed the H&S behaviors in daily activities.

10. Design a coaching program to train coaches, to follow up on your H&S cultural change program.

11. Track the number and quality of coaching conversations that happen as a result.

 Action focus 15

For senior managers:
Ask your H&S teams whether you can be coached on leading the new H&S behaviors.

For health and safety professionals:
Design a self-assessment exercise to be used with the new H&S behaviors.

For the communications and engagement manager:
Help the H&S team create a conversation technique for H&S intervention.

For the HR director:
Find out whether any existing coaching program in the company could be leveraged for health and safety.

Ruth Denyer, safety director

Health and safety is part of a bigger issue: the issue of risk. I only understood this fully when I took on risk management roles, which included health and safety as one of the risks that I needed to manage, and realized that a broader approach – looking at health and safety from a risk standpoint – was really useful.

What I also realized is that other risks were being managed company-wide, so why was health and safety left to a standalone department or function? Why was it not being managed across the company, like other risks such as financial, reputational and business continuity? We reached out to the London School of Economics and looked into their work on the psychology of risk.

With risk, there is no perfect solution, no good answer, because risk can never be eliminated. It means taking decisions and making choices, and we often need to ask ourselves "What is the 'least bad' choice?" It is about devolving responsibility for health and safety to the entire company and getting everyone involved. After all, it is only the people who own the work activity who can make a decision about the risk involved in it.

It is about making sure that we are having the right conversations. Instead of asking "What is the cost of compliance?" we need to ask "What does success look like?" and then "What are you willing to risk to achieve it?" In this way, we manage health and safety in a way that delivers best value to the business. It also allows us to understand why we are doing it. When people have a strong 'why,' they are motivated to get involved.

While the legislation and what we need to do to comply is important, if we focus purely on this, it may distract us from what the business needs. We will also fail to consider the human element, which is often the thing that drives us to do, and be, better at health and safety – and at everything.

What works best, then, is to embed the H&S conversation into the broader risk conversations and get everyone to have them, at all levels of the company. In companies where I have worked, we have had some in-depth conversations about risk in our leadership training. To discuss and make decisions about risk, you really do need to understand the issues and have considered all possibilities.

It is also important that we have these H&S conversations early on, at the planning stage of all our activities, otherwise managing our H&S risk will cost us more. This means we won't do it effectively and we may put our people at risk. When we get everyone involved, we create a culture of ownership for health and safety. This is where approaching health and safety, as part of the overall process of managing our risk, really works, because then it simply becomes part of what we do.

This is important because we cannot have an H&S culture – to support health and safety – *and* another culture to support our business. They have to be the same thing if the company is going to function effectively and manage its risks in the process.

Diagram 4 – Build, Buzz, Bake – a recipe for transformational health and safety.

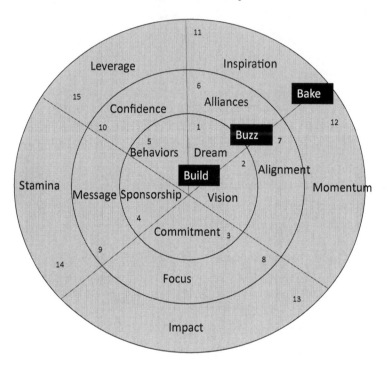

What now?

If you have got to the end of this book, then I know you are ready.

Keeping health and safety front of mind in companies is a constant struggle, and I can't promise the journey you are about to embark upon will be easy.

Like an extremely large jigsaw, there will be lots of different pieces, and at times the task will seem so daunting you will want to give up.

With a good set of instructions, however, and all the important pieces of the puzzle available to you, I am confident that you will find the rightful place for every single piece. I can already see you basking in the afterglow of a big challenge tackled and overcome.

The main pieces of the jigsaw have been outlined in this book, and even if new pieces appear, I hope that having read this book will help you to figure out where to put them.

So, let's recap on those jigsaw pieces right now.

Remember we are completing this jigsaw in three parts:

Part 1 – BUILD

This is where we set an ambitious vision for our company, to make health and safety a strategic focus, a competitive strategy even. Then, once we are sure the vision is big enough, we set about laying the foundations for success. We get our entire management team on board, build key alliances across the company and get ready to challenge the status quo. Arguably this process is where our change effort is won or lost, so we must give it the time and attention it needs.

Part 2 – BUZZ

This is where all our key change management skills come in. It is also from where our change effort will get launched, with a big buzz around it. Here we start to influence, persuade and inspire. We will be training others to help us and putting transformational leadership at the heart of everything we do. Being in this phase can be exhilarating, as employees revel in the novelty of our approach, and talk about it excitedly. Our challenge at this stage is turning quick wins into long-term gains.

Part 3 – BAKE

During the final phase, with its three watchwords of consistency, constancy and reach, only having these things in spadefuls will enable our change effort to gain momentum, traction and eventually, integration. Once our program messages and behaviors become integrated into daily work activities and key business processes, sustainability is guaranteed.

At all times we need to keep in the forefront of our minds the reasons why we are doing this.

The main reason is for the people we work with, and the people around us, who all deserve to go home as safe and well as they arrived at work.

No one sets out to be an accident statistic, or to be the instigator of one, but these things still happen, to the tune of 693,000 people sustaining a non-fatal injury at work in the UK in 2019/20.[25]

This is the main reason that we need to lead our company health and safety first, but as this book has outlined, the other reasons are endless.

The three phases outlined in this book offer a comprehensive guide to setting up, implementing and sustaining an H&S leadership program that has the potential to transform not only our company's health and safety performance, but its business performance overall. According to research by Krause and Bell in 2015,[26] safe companies are also high-performing companies, which is everyone's goal.

If you are an HR or communications person reading this, and already have a successful leadership or engagement program, then why not consider extending it to include health and safety, and to all employees? That way you can bring out the leadership potential in everyone. This has the potential to transform the company by using health and safety – something that everyone can get involved in – as a lever.

If you are a senior manager or health and safety director reading this, and you already have an H&S leadership program in place, which isn't quite getting the traction you had hoped for, use the 'Build, Buzz, Bake' formula and its component parts as a checklist. Maybe there is something in here to give your program the reboot it needs.

Whatever your role or objective, reading this book is only the start of the journey. Once you start to implement its recommendations, you should feel confident that you are caring for your employees, as well as creating a ripple effect, which will be hard to stop.

That feeling of health, safety and being cared for will lead to levels of engagement the company can harness – not just for health and safety, but for other important issues as well.

The culture you build for health and safety, and the leadership skills you generate, will be key to your company's long-term success, no matter what the external and internal challenges.

As I have said before, and will no doubt say again many times, "If you can lead on health and safety, you can lead on anything."

So, fasten your seatbelt and get ready for the ride.

It is time for you to breathe new life into the *old* health and safety and get your people so fired up that they not only take ownership of health and safety, but every other challenge in your business as well.

It's time for health and safety levership – through people power!

Endnotes

1. Pfeffer, J. (2018) *Dying for a Paycheck*, New York, Harper Collins.

2. Bersin, J. (2021) *HR Predictions for 2021 Report*, Josh Bersin Academy.

3. CIPD (2021) *Health and wellbeing at work 2021: Survey report*, London, Chartered Institute of Personnel and Development.

4. Gawande, A. A. (2009) *The Checklist Manifesto: How to get things right*, New York, Henry Holt and Company.

5. Covey, S. (1989) *The 7 Habits of Highly Effective People*, New York, Free Press.

6. Kotter, J. and Rathgeber, H. (2017) *Our Iceberg Is Melting*, Basingstoke, Macmillan.

7. Sinek, S. (2019) *The Infinite Game: How Great Businesses Achieve Long-Lasting Success*, Portfolio Penguin.

8. Parker, D., Lawrie, M. and Hudson, P. (2006) "A framework for understanding the development of company safety culture," *Safety Science*, vol. 44, no. 6, pp. 551–562.

9. Bennis, W. and Nanus, B. (1985) *Leaders: Strategies for Taking Charge*, New York, Harper & Row.

10. Coué, E. (2017) *Self-Mastery Through Conscious Autosuggestion*, Musaicum Books.

11. Miller, G. A. (1956) "The Magical Number Seven, Plus or Minus Two: Some Limits on Our Capacity for Processing Information," *Psychological Review*.

12. Meyer, E. and Hastings, R. (2020) *No Rules: Netflix and the Culture of Reinvention*, London, W. H. Allen.

13. Pink, D. H. (2010) *Drive: The Surprising Truth About What Motivates Us*, Canongate Books.

14. Charvet, S. R. (2019) *Words that Change Minds: The 14 patterns for mastering the language of influence*, Success Strategies.

15. Barling, J., Loughlin, C. and Kelloway, E. K. (2002) 'Development and test of a model linking safety-specific transformational leadership and occupational safety', *Journal of Applied Psychology*, vol. 87, no.3, pp. 488–496.

16. McGregor Burns, J. (1978) *Leadership*, New York, Harper & Row.

17. Duhigg, C. (2012) *The Power of Habit: Why We Do What We Do in Life and Business*, Random House.

18. Thaler, R. H. and Sunstein, C. R. (2009) *Nudge: Improving Decisions about Health, Wealth and Happiness*, Yale University Press.

19. Delizonna, L. (2017) 'High-Performing Teams need Psychological Safety. Here's how to create it', *Harvard Business Review* [Online]. Available at https://hbr.org/2017/08/high-performing-teams-need-psychological-safety-heres-how-to-create-it (Accessed 7 June 2021).

20. Collins, J. (2001) *Good to Great: Why Some Companies Make the Leap ... and Others Don't*, Random House Business.

21. McKinsey (2021) 'Psychological safety and the critical role of leadership development', London, McKinsey & Company [Online]. Available at https://www.mckinsey.com/business-functions/organization/our-insights/psychological-safety-and-the-critical-role-of-leadership-development (Accessed 26 May 2021).

22. Deming, W. E. (1993) *The New Economics for Industry, Government and Education*, Boston, MIT Press.

23. Kirkpatrick, D. L. (1998) *Evaluating Training Programs: The Four Levels*, 2nd edn, Jossey Bass.

24. Bungay Stanier, M. (2016) *The Coaching Habit: Say Less; Ask More & Change the Way You Lead Forever*, Box of Crayons Press.

25. HSE (2020) *Health and safety at work. Summary statistics for Great Britain 2020.* [Online]. Available at https://www.hse.gov.uk/statistics/

overall/hssh1920.pdf (Accessed 7 June 2021).

26. Krause, T. R. and Bell, K. J. (2015) *7 Insights into Safety Leadership*, chapter 1, The Safety Leadership Institute.

About the Author

Karen J. Hewitt uses health and safety to transform the cultures of large, complex companies. She has spent the last ten years creating leadership movements, and growing engagement in companies that have decided that focusing on worker health and safety is not only the right thing to do, but also makes good business sense.

Karen is fluent in five European languages, and uses them to increase the global reach of her movements. She brings a unique skillset of communications, leadership, linguistics and learning design to the H&S function of a company and is an H&S professional in her own right. With her analytical skills, customer focus and knowledge of human behavior, she can transform the way employees engage with health and safety, and boost company engagement levels across the board.

The transformational leadership and engagement principles that Karen advocates apply equally well to other business areas, not just health and safety. Her first book, *Employee Confidence: The New rules of Engagement*, published in 2018, is a No.1 Amazon bestseller and was a finalist in the leadership category of the Business Book Awards, 2019.

Karen is also a certified yoga teacher and a trainer of neurolinguistic programming and hypnosis. She lives in the meditative surrounds of Berkshire with partner David, daughter Mila, a garden, a log cabin, three frogs and a sandpit.